The Peloponnesian War Chronicles: Power, Politics, and Conflict in Ancient Greece

The Peloponnesian War Chronicles, Volume 1

Christoffer Smestad

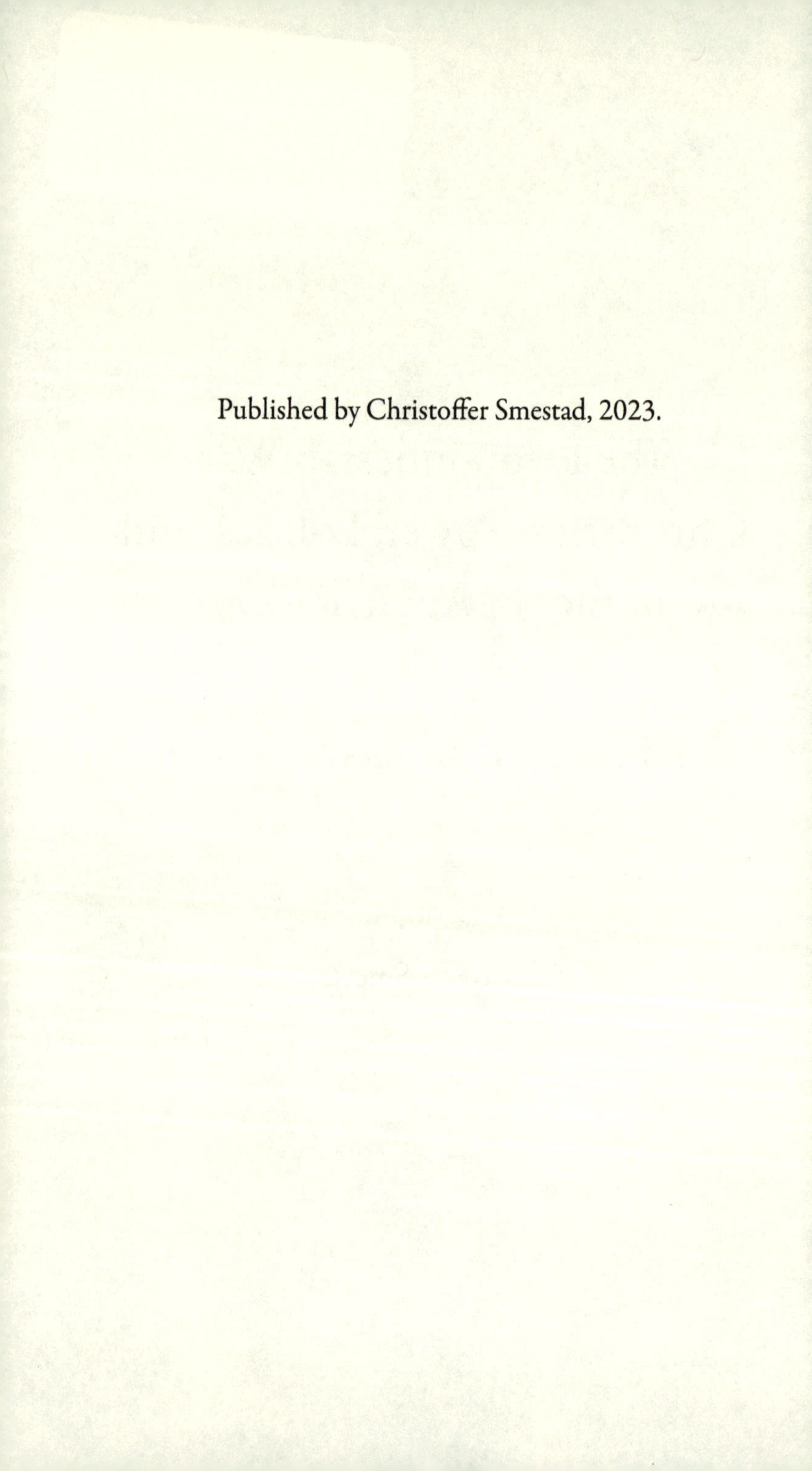

Published by Christoffer Smestad, 2023.

While every precaution has been taken in the preparation of this book, the publisher assumes no responsibility for errors or omissions, or for damages resulting from the use of the information contained herein.

THE PELOPONNESIAN WAR CHRONICLES: POWER, POLITICS, AND CONFLICT IN ANCIENT GREECE

First edition. May 30, 2023.

ISBN: 979-8223603313

Written by Christoffer Smestad.

Table of Contents

Chapter 1: Introduction to the Peloponnesian War: Historical Context and Key Players

Introduction: The Peloponnesian War stands as one of the most significant and impactful conflicts in ancient Greek history. This chapter sets the stage for our exploration of the war by providing an overview of its historical context and introducing the key players involved.

1.1 The Pre-War Greek World: To understand the origins of the Peloponnesian War, we must first examine the Greek world leading up to the conflict. Greece was comprised of numerous city-states, each with its own unique political system, alliances, and ambitions. Two prominent city-states emerged as the main contenders: Athens and Sparta.

The Greek world was a dynamic and diverse collection of city-states, known as polis, spread across the mainland and islands. These city-states varied in size, population, and political structure. Some notable examples besides Athens and Sparta include Corinth, Thebes, Argos, and Syracuse.

Athens, located in the region of Attica, was a democratic city-state that stood out for its political system. Under the leadership of statesmen such as Pericles, Athens established a direct democracy where eligible citizens had a say in the decision-making process. This allowed for active civic participation and the flourishing of democratic ideals.

Sparta, situated in the region of Laconia, contrasted with Athens in its political and social organization. Sparta operated under a unique system known as the dual monarchy, with two kings ruling jointly. Alongside the kings, there was a council of elders and an assembly of citizens. Sparta's society revolved around military discipline, emphasizing physical training and the cultivation of virtues such as courage and self-sacrifice.

As Athens and Sparta grew in power and influence, they emerged as the leading city-states and the main contenders for dominance in the Greek world. Their differing political systems and societal values contributed to a stark contrast between the two powers. Athens boasted its cultural achievements, naval prowess, and democratic ideals, while Sparta prided itself on its military might, discipline, and adherence to traditional values.

Both Athens and Sparta formed alliances with other city-states to bolster their positions and pursue their respective ambitions. Athens led the Delian League, which initially aimed to protect Greek city-states from Persian threats but gradually transformed into an Athenian-dominated alliance, extending Athens' influence and control. Sparta, on the other hand, spearheaded the Peloponnesian League, comprising city-states within the Peloponnese region, with the goal of maintaining Spartan hegemony and countering Athenian power.

The distinct political systems, alliances, and ambitions of Athens and Sparta set the stage for the Peloponnesian War. As these two prominent city-states vied for dominance, the tensions and rivalries between them escalated, eventually leading to a devastating and protracted conflict that would shape the course of Greek history.

1.2 Athens: Rise of a Naval Power:

Athens, known for its democratic government and vibrant intellectual and cultural life, underwent a remarkable transformation under the leadership of statesmen such as Pericles. It emerged as a dominant naval power and established the Delian League, an alliance of city-states centered around Athens, which gradually evolved into an Athenian empire.

Under the guidance of visionary leaders like Pericles, Athens experienced a period of unprecedented growth and influence. The Athenians recognized the strategic advantage of their location near the sea and embarked on an ambitious naval expansion. They constructed a formidable fleet known as the Athenian triremes, sleek warships powered by rowers, which became the backbone of their naval supremacy.

With its powerful navy, Athens effectively projected its influence beyond its borders. The establishment of the Delian League in 478 BC, initially formed as a defensive alliance against Persian threats, marked a turning point in Athenian foreign policy. The member city-states contributed resources, usually in the form of money or ships, to a common treasury located on the island of Delos. However, over time, Athens gradually transformed the alliance into an Athenian empire, exerting control over the member states and using their resources to enhance its own power and wealth.

The Athenian empire, built on naval dominance and the economic contributions of its allies, allowed Athens to maintain a vast network of trade and exert influence over key maritime routes. This newfound power provided Athens with economic prosperity, enabling the city-state to invest in public infrastructure, cultural achievements, and the beautification of the city, as exemplified by the construction of the Parthenon atop the Acropolis.

1.3 Sparta: The Military Hegemon:

Sparta, with its disciplined society and formidable land-based military, was Athens' main rival. It led the Peloponnesian League, a coalition of city-states in the Peloponnese region. Spartan society prioritized military training and adherence to strict social norms.

Unlike Athens, which embraced democratic principles and fostered a cultural and intellectual environment, Sparta adhered to a militaristic way of life. From an early age, Spartan citizens, known as Spartiates, underwent rigorous military training, emphasizing physical endurance, discipline, and obedience. The Spartan army, renowned for its highly trained hoplites, formed the backbone of Sparta's military dominance in mainland Greece.

Spartan society revolved around the notion of communal well-being and the preservation of a unique way of life known as the Spartan "ideal." Social norms were strictly enforced, discouraging individualism and emphasizing the collective strength of the state. Spartiates were expected to prioritize the needs of the state above personal ambitions, and even matters such as marriage and family were regulated to ensure the continuation of a strong and disciplined society.

As the leader of the Peloponnesian League, Sparta sought to maintain its hegemony and counterbalance the growing power of Athens. The city-state formed alliances with other Peloponnesian city-states, reinforcing its military might and solidifying its position as the dominant land-based power in Greece.

The contrasting ideologies of Athens and Sparta, with Athens emphasizing naval power, cultural achievements, and democratic principles, and Sparta emphasizing military prowess, discipline, and adherence to social norms, laid the foundation for the fierce rivalry and eventual clash that would erupt in the Peloponnesian War.

1.4 The Seeds of Conflict: Tensions between Athens and Sparta

Tensions between Athens and Sparta simmered for years before erupting into open conflict. Divergent ideologies, political ambitions, and the competition for dominance in Greece contributed to the rising animosity between the two powers. Friction between their respective allies, such as Corinth and Megara, further fueled the flames.

The contrasting ideologies and political systems of Athens and Sparta played a significant role in the emergence of tension. Athens, with its democratic principles and focus on naval power, sought to expand its influence and establish an empire that would safeguard its interests. The Athenians believed in the power of their democratic institutions and cultural superiority, which sometimes led to a sense of arrogance and a willingness to assert their dominance over other city-states.

On the other hand, Sparta, with its military-based society and conservative values, was wary of Athens' growing power. Sparta viewed itself as the guardian of traditional Greek values and saw Athens' imperial ambitions as a threat to the existing order. Spartan leaders feared that Athenian influence and dominance could undermine their own power and way of life.

Competition for dominance in Greece was another key factor in the escalation of tensions. Both Athens and Sparta aspired to be the preeminent power in Greece, with each city-state seeking to expand its sphere of influence and gain the support of other city-states. As Athens' empire grew through the Delian League, many city-states became subject to Athenian control, causing resentment and resistance among those who felt subjugated.

The actions and policies of Athens and Sparta's respective allies also played a role in exacerbating the tensions. Corinth, a prominent member of the Peloponnesian League and a staunch opponent of Athens, actively worked to undermine Athenian influence and influence other city-states to join their cause. Megara, a city-state with close ties to Corinth, also became embroiled in the conflict, as it faced economic sanctions from Athens, leading to further animosity between the two powers.

As these tensions continued to mount, diplomatic efforts to mitigate conflicts and maintain peace ultimately failed. The stage was set for open hostilities, and the seeds of the Peloponnesian War were sown. The coming chapters will delve into the events leading up to the outbreak of the war and the subsequent military campaigns and political maneuvers that defined this significant conflict in ancient Greek history.

1.5 The Immediate Cause: Dispute over Corcyra and the Escalation to War

While underlying tensions existed, the immediate cause of the Peloponnesian War was a dispute between Athens and Corinth over their respective influences in the city-state of Corcyra (modern-day Corfu). This conflict, which initially seemed localized, eventually drew in their allies and escalated into a full-scale war.

Corcyra, a strategically important island situated in the Ionian Sea, held significant naval power and had ties with both Athens and Corinth. The city-state's position as a naval powerhouse made it a coveted ally for both sides. Corinth, fearing Athenian expansion and seeking to maintain its own influence, sought to secure Corcyra's allegiance. Athens, keen on preventing Corinth from gaining control over such a valuable ally, intervened in the conflict.

Athens' intervention in the Corcyraean dispute was a pivotal moment that transformed a regional conflict into a wider war. By siding with Corcyra, Athens signaled its determination to uphold its imperial ambitions and maintain its dominance in the Greek world. Corinth, feeling threatened by Athens' involvement, called upon its allies within the Peloponnesian League, primarily Sparta, to respond to what they perceived as an Athenian aggression.

The involvement of allies on both sides quickly escalated the conflict. Sparta, as the leader of the Peloponnesian League and the main adversary of Athens, felt compelled to defend Corinth's interests and challenge the expanding influence of Athens. Other city-states within the Greek world, driven by their own political interests and concerns, aligned themselves with either Athens or Sparta, further solidifying the division and setting the stage for a larger conflict.

The dispute over Corcyra was not merely a localized conflict, but rather a catalyst that triggered the war between Athens and Sparta, drawing their respective allies into the fray. The deeper-rooted tensions and rivalries between the two powers, combined with the quest for dominance in the Greek world, erupted into a protracted and devastating conflict that would shape the course of Greek history for years to come.

1.6 Other Players: The War Involving Greek City-States

While Athens and Sparta took center stage, the Peloponnesian War involved a range of other Greek city-states. These included Thebes, Corinth, Megara, Argos, and others, each with its own motivations, alliances, and strategies. The involvement of these city-states added complexity and depth to the conflict.

Thebes, a powerful city-state located in Boeotia, emerged as a significant player during the Peloponnesian War. Thebes had its own ambitions and sought to increase its influence within the Greek world. Initially, Thebes aligned itself with Sparta, viewing the Athenian empire as a threat. However, as the war progressed and circumstances evolved, Thebes shifted its allegiances, at times siding with Athens against Sparta and vice versa, strategically maneuvering to protect its own interests.

Corinth, a leading member of the Peloponnesian League and a staunch opponent of Athens, played a pivotal role in the conflict. Corinth viewed Athens as a threat to its commercial interests and its regional power. The Corinthian city-state actively sought alliances and support from other city-states, such as Megara and Thebes, to counter Athenian influence. Corinth's antagonism towards Athens fueled the flames of war and influenced other city-states to take a more active role in the conflict.

Megara, located near Athens, faced economic sanctions imposed by Athens, which strained its relations with the Athenian empire. Megara, seeking to free itself from Athenian control and regain its independence, aligned itself with Sparta and became an active participant in the war. Megara's involvement added another layer of complexity to the conflict, as it highlighted the economic and political rivalries between city-states and their efforts to resist Athenian dominance.

Argos, a major city-state in the northeastern Peloponnese, also became involved in the war, albeit with a different agenda. Argos saw an opportunity to challenge Sparta's hegemony in the region and sought to weaken its rival. Argos formed alliances with Athens and other city-states, aiming to exploit the ongoing conflict to its advantage and expand its own influence.

Other Greek city-states, though not as prominently featured, also played a role in the war. Some, like Syracuse in Sicily, were drawn into the conflict due to their alliances or geopolitical interests. Others, such as Thessaly and Euboea, were strategic territories that served as battlegrounds or pawns in the larger power struggles between Athens and Sparta.

The involvement of these city-states added complexity and diversity to the Peloponnesian War. Each city-state had its own motivations, alliances, and strategies, contributing to the ever-shifting dynamics of the conflict. The war was not merely a clash between Athens and Sparta but a complex web of alliances, rivalries, and ambitions that encompassed the entire Greek world.

1.7 Thucydides and the Historiography of the War: Thucydides, a Historical Source

The primary historical account of the Peloponnesian War comes from Thucydides, an Athenian general who witnessed and chronicled the events. Thucydides' work, known as "The History of the Peloponnesian War," stands as a valuable source for understanding this significant conflict.

Thucydides, unlike many historians of his time, approached his work with a desire for accuracy and a commitment to providing an impartial account of the war. He sought to uncover the underlying causes and motivations of the conflict, as well as the political and military strategies employed by the various city-states involved. Thucydides' narrative is characterized by his meticulous attention to detail, his reliance on eyewitness testimonies, and his analytical approach to interpreting events.

Thucydides' work is not merely a straightforward chronicle of battles and political maneuvers but a deeper exploration of the human nature and the forces that drive nations to war. He delves into the psychological aspects of warfare, the impact of power dynamics on decision-making, and the consequences of conflict on society. Thucydides' keen observations and insights provide readers with a nuanced understanding of the complexities of the war and its far-reaching implications.

The significance of Thucydides' account lies not only in its historical accuracy but also in its enduring influence on the field of historiography. His work laid the foundation for the modern study of history, characterized by a commitment to factual evidence, rigorous analysis, and a critical examination of multiple perspectives. Thucydides' approach to historical writing set a standard for subsequent historians, shaping the discipline for centuries to come.

While Thucydides' account serves as a primary historical source, it is important to acknowledge that his perspective, despite his efforts at objectivity, was influenced by his Athenian background and personal experiences. His account may reflect a bias towards Athens, and certain events or individuals may be emphasized or downplayed based on his own judgments. Therefore, it is essential to approach his work with a critical eye and supplement it with other historical sources to gain a comprehensive understanding of the war.

In conclusion, the Peloponnesian War was a conflict deeply rooted in the political, military, and cultural dynamics of ancient Greece. Athens and Sparta, as the main contenders, shaped the course of the war with their contrasting strengths and ideologies. Understanding the historical context, key players, and the significance of Thucydides' account provides a solid foundation for comprehending the causes, events, and consequences of this transformative period in ancient Greek history.

Chapter 2: The Rise of Athens and Sparta: A Comparison of the Two City-States' Strengths and Weaknesses

Introduction: To fully grasp the dynamics of the Peloponnesian War, it is essential to explore the strengths and weaknesses of the two major players: Athens and Sparta. This chapter offers a comparative analysis of the rise of these city-states, examining their respective strengths and vulnerabilities that shaped their roles in the conflict.

2.1 Athens: The Naval Powerhouse

2.1.1 Democratic Government and Political Structure:

Athens, the prominent city-state during the Peloponnesian War, was known for its unique democratic system of government. Unlike other city-states that were ruled by kings or oligarchies, Athens placed power in the hands of its citizens.

In Athens, all male citizens above a certain age had the right to participate in the political process. They gathered in the Assembly, the principal democratic institution, where they could debate and vote on important matters such as legislation, foreign policy decisions, and the election of officials. The Assembly was a crucial platform for citizens to express their opinions and shape the direction of Athenian governance.

Additionally, Athens had a system of popular courts where citizens served as jurors. They would listen to arguments, examine evidence, and render verdicts in legal cases. This democratic participation in the judicial process provided a sense of civic responsibility and ensured that citizens had a direct role in upholding justice.

The Athenian political structure fostered a strong sense of civic engagement and unity among its citizens. It encouraged active involvement in public affairs, creating a sense of ownership and collective responsibility for the well-being and success of the city-state. The democratic system also helped to cultivate a spirit of innovation, as diverse voices and perspectives could contribute to the decision-making process.

The Athenian democracy, however, was not without its limitations. Only a fraction of the population enjoyed full political rights, as women, slaves, and foreign residents were excluded from citizenship and the democratic process. Nonetheless, the democratic government of Athens was a defining feature of the city-state and played a significant role in shaping its identity as a naval powerhouse.

2.1.2 Naval Superiority:

Athens' naval strength was a key factor in its rise as a dominant power in the Greek world. The Athenians recognized the strategic importance of maritime capabilities and invested significant resources in building a formidable navy.

The Athenian navy, known as the "Athenian Trireme Fleet," consisted of triremes, sleek and fast warships propelled by three banks of oars. These ships were manned by skilled rowers and armed with marines, enabling Athens to project its power across the Aegean Sea and beyond.

The naval superiority of Athens provided several advantages. It allowed the city-state to protect its trade routes, maintain control over its colonies and allies, and exert influence over other city-states. The Athenian navy also played a crucial role in the defense of Athens itself, as it could effectively transport troops and supplies and provide a strong defense against seaborne attacks.

Furthermore, Athens utilized its naval power to establish the Delian League, an alliance of city-states that initially formed for mutual defense against Persia. Over time, however, Athens gradually transformed the Delian League into an Athenian empire. Through the Delian League, Athens controlled a network of allies and tribute-paying states, further consolidating its naval dominance and expanding its political influence.

The naval strength of Athens not only secured its maritime interests but also bolstered its political and economic power. The ability to project force across the seas and maintain a powerful navy set Athens apart from its rivals and positioned it as a dominant force in the Greek world.

2.1.3 Naval Dominance and the Delian League: Athens developed a formidable navy, which became the backbone of its military might. The creation of the Delian League enabled Athens to expand its influence and establish control over a vast network of allied city-states and resources.

2.1.4 Commercial and Economic Strength: The Athenian Empire brought economic prosperity. Athens was a hub of trade and commerce, benefiting from its access to ports, resources, and tributes from its allies. Its wealth funded grand construction projects and fueled its military endeavors.

2.2 Sparta: The Military Hegemon 2.2.1 Social Structure and Military Training: Sparta's society was defined by its military focus and strict social hierarchy. Its citizens, known as Spartiates, underwent rigorous military training from a young age, instilling discipline, endurance, and cohesion among its forces.

2.2.2 Land-Based Military Supremacy: Sparta's hoplite phalanx, consisting of heavily armored infantry, was renowned for its effectiveness in battle. Spartan warriors, disciplined and highly skilled, formed an almost unbeatable force on land.

2.2.3 Political Stability and Oligarchic Government: Sparta's political structure was characterized by its dual kingship and a council of elders. This oligarchic system provided stability and efficient decision-making, ensuring a united front during times of conflict.

2.2.4 Agricultural Economy and Self-Sufficiency: Sparta's economy relied heavily on agriculture. Its fertile lands and helot laborers provided a steady supply of food, allowing Spartan citizens to focus primarily on military matters. This self-sufficiency bolstered Sparta's resilience.

2.3 Strengths and Weaknesses in Comparison

2.3.1 Athenian Weaknesses:

While Athens boasted significant strengths, it also had notable weaknesses that affected its position in the Peloponnesian War.

Lack of military prowess on land compared to Sparta: Athens excelled in naval warfare but lacked the same level of expertise and dominance on land as its rival, Sparta. The Athenian military, while formidable at sea, faced challenges when engaging in large-scale land battles. This limitation made it difficult for Athens to directly challenge Sparta's land-based forces and posed a significant obstacle in achieving decisive victories on land.

Reliance on naval superiority: Athens heavily relied on its naval supremacy as the cornerstone of its military strategy. The Athenian Trireme Fleet provided the city-state with the ability to project power across the sea, protect its maritime interests, and exert influence over its allies and colonies. However, this reliance on naval superiority also made Athens vulnerable. If the Athenian navy suffered significant losses or faced effective countermeasures by its enemies, it could undermine Athens' military capabilities and weaken its overall position in the war.

Vulnerability to disease outbreaks: The dense population within the walls of Athens created an environment conducive to the spread of diseases. During the war, Athens faced a devastating epidemic known as the Plague of Athens, which resulted in a significant loss of life and weakened the city's ability to sustain its military campaigns. The outbreak of diseases, such as the plague, exposed the vulnerability of

Athens' crowded urban environment, impacting its military effectiveness and overall stability.

These weaknesses placed Athens at a disadvantage in certain aspects of the war. However, it is important to note that Athens also possessed significant strengths, such as its democratic government, naval prowess, and intellectual and cultural achievements. The dynamic interplay between these strengths and weaknesses, along with the strategies employed by Athens, Sparta, and other city-states, shaped the course and outcome of the Peloponnesian War.

While Sparta was a formidable military power with its renowned land-based forces, it also had certain weaknesses that influenced its position in the Peloponnesian War.

Limited naval capabilities: Unlike Athens, Sparta did not possess a strong naval tradition nor the resources to build a significant fleet. This limitation made it difficult for Sparta to challenge Athens' dominance at sea. The inability to match Athens' naval power hindered Sparta's ability to project force across the Aegean and limit Athens' control over its allies and colonies. This naval disadvantage confined Sparta's military operations primarily to land-based campaigns.

Dependency on agriculture: Spartan society was largely agrarian, with a heavy reliance on the cultivation of land for sustenance. This agricultural focus restricted Sparta's capacity for long-term warfare or sustained campaigns far from their homeland. Unlike Athens, which had a diverse economy and access to overseas trade, Sparta faced limitations in terms of resource mobilization and provisioning its armies for extended periods. These constraints affected Sparta's ability to engage in prolonged conflicts and exert its influence beyond the Peloponnese region.

Potential reluctance from some allies: While Sparta led the Peloponnesian League, a coalition of city-states in the Peloponnese region, its dominance and perceived harsh treatment of its allies could lead to reluctance and discontent among some of them. The hegemonic nature of Spartan rule and its emphasis on maintaining strict social norms could create tensions and resentment among other city-states. This could undermine Sparta's ability to maintain a cohesive alliance and garner full support from its allies in the war effort.

These weaknesses, combined with Sparta's strengths such as its formidable land-based military and disciplined society, shaped its role and strategies during the Peloponnesian War. The interplay between these strengths and weaknesses, along with the actions and strategies of Athens and other city-states, contributed to the complex dynamics of the conflict.

Conclusion: Athens and Sparta emerged as dominant powers in ancient Greece, each with distinct strengths and weaknesses. Athens thrived through its democratic government, cultural brilliance, naval supremacy, and economic prosperity. In contrast, Sparta excelled in its militaristic society, land-based military prowess, political stability, and agricultural self-sufficiency. Understanding these divergent strengths and vulnerabilities lays the groundwork for comprehending the strategies and outcomes of the Peloponnesian War, which we will explore in subsequent chapters.

Chapter 3: The Origins of Conflict: Tensions between Athens and Sparta Prior to the War

Introduction: Before the outbreak of the Peloponnesian War, tensions simmered between Athens and Sparta. This chapter delves into the origins of the conflict, exploring the underlying causes and key events that strained the relationship between the two city-states.

3.1 Territorial Disputes:

The territorial disputes between Athens and Sparta were a significant contributing factor to the tensions that ultimately led to the outbreak of the Peloponnesian War. The geographical proximity of the two city-states, combined with their aspirations for regional dominance, fueled conflicts and rivalries over control of neighboring territories.

Athens, as the leader of the Delian League, gradually expanded its influence and established a network of allies and colonies throughout the Aegean Sea. This expansion brought Athens into direct contact with other city-states, including those within the Peloponnese region, which was traditionally considered Spartan territory. The growing power and territorial ambitions of Athens posed a challenge to Sparta's regional dominance and led to increasing friction between the two powers.

One notable territorial dispute involved the city-state of Megara. Megara, located strategically between Athens and the Peloponnese, was initially an ally of Athens. However, tensions arose when Megara decided to break away from the Delian League and align itself with the Peloponnesian League led by Sparta. This move threatened Athens' control over Megara and its access to the Isthmus of Corinth, a crucial land route connecting the Peloponnese to the rest of Greece. The conflict over Megara escalated and became one of the catalysts for the outbreak of the Peloponnesian War.

Another contentious issue was the control of various islands and city-states in the Aegean Sea. Both Athens and Sparta sought to expand their influence and secure important strategic positions in these regions. This led to clashes and confrontations as each city-state attempted to assert its control over key territories, often resulting in localized conflicts and diplomatic tensions.

The territorial disputes between Athens and Sparta were not limited to specific regions but extended across the Greek world. As the two main contenders for dominance, they competed for control over various city-states, islands, and trade routes, which created a volatile atmosphere and a constant risk of conflict.

The underlying territorial disputes, coupled with the broader political and ideological differences between Athens and Sparta, set the stage for the Peloponnesian War. The clash of interests and the struggle for territorial control played a significant role in shaping the course and outcome of the war.

3.2 Megara and Corinth:

The city-states of Megara and Corinth played significant roles in the escalating tensions between Athens and Sparta, contributing to the dynamics of the Peloponnesian War. Both Megara and Corinth held close ties with Sparta and resented Athens' expanding power and influence in the region.

Megara, strategically located between Athens and the Peloponnese, held a complex position in the conflict. Initially, Megara was an ally and important trade partner of Athens. However, as tensions between Athens and Sparta grew, Megara decided to break away from the Delian League and align itself with the Peloponnesian League led by Sparta. This shift in allegiance challenged Athens' control over Megara and posed a threat to its access to the Isthmus of Corinth, a crucial land route connecting the Peloponnese to the rest of Greece. The conflict over Megara intensified as both Athens and Sparta sought to assert their influence over the city-state, ultimately contributing to the outbreak of the war.

Corinth, another prominent member of the Peloponnesian League, played a pivotal role in the conflict. Corinth resented Athens' growing power and sought to challenge its influence in the region. The city-state of Corinth had its own aspirations for regional dominance and saw Athens as a major obstacle to achieving its goals. Corinth's alliance with Sparta and its efforts to rally other city-states against Athens further exacerbated the tensions between the two sides.

Corinth's grievances against Athens extended beyond mere territorial disputes. Corinth accused Athens of economic exploitation, citing instances where Athens had interfered with Corinthian trade and imposed unfair restrictions on its commerce. These economic grievances, combined with political and ideological differences, fueled Corinth's animosity towards Athens and contributed to its active involvement in the Peloponnesian War.

The actions and alliances of Megara and Corinth, as important players in the conflict, significantly influenced the course and outcome of the Peloponnesian War. Their alignment with Sparta and their efforts to challenge Athens' power added to the complexity and intensity of the conflict, shaping the strategies and decisions made by both sides. The involvement of Megara and Corinth highlights the intricate web of alliances, rivalries, and regional dynamics that characterized the Peloponnesian War.

3.3 The Megarian Decree:

In 432 BC, Athens enacted the Megarian Decree, a significant event that heightened tensions between Athens and Sparta, and played a role in the escalation towards the Peloponnesian War. The Megarian Decree was a unilateral economic sanction imposed by Athens on the city-state of Megara, a key ally of Sparta.

The Megarian Decree aimed to cripple Megara's economy by prohibiting Megarian merchants from trading with the Athenian Empire and its allied territories. This move was a direct response to Megara's decision to break away from the Delian League and align itself with Sparta. Athens saw Megara's alignment with Sparta as a threat to its interests and as an act of betrayal.

The economic sanctions imposed by the Megarian Decree had severe consequences for Megara. As a significant trading partner of Athens, Megara heavily relied on its trade relations with the Athenian Empire for its economic well-being. The Megarian Decree effectively cut off Megara from accessing vital markets and resources within the Athenian Empire, severely impacting its commerce and overall prosperity.

The Megarian Decree not only targeted Megara but also aimed to exert pressure on Sparta by disrupting its economic ties with its ally. By isolating Megara economically, Athens sought to undermine Megara's support for Sparta and weaken the Peloponnesian League.

The enactment of the Megarian Decree was seen as a provocative and aggressive move by Athens. It was viewed by Sparta and its allies as a direct threat to Megara's welfare and its alliance with Sparta. The economic sanctions deepened the animosity between Athens and Sparta, further polarizing the two city-states and fueling the flames of conflict.

The Megarian Decree, while seemingly a targeted economic measure, had broader implications. It symbolized the growing hostilities between Athens and Sparta and highlighted the use of economic means as a weapon in the power struggle between the two powers. The decree contributed to the deteriorating relations between the Athenian Empire and the Peloponnesian League, ultimately playing a part in the outbreak of the Peloponnesian War.

3.4 The Corcyraean Conflict:

The conflict between Corcyra (Corfu) and Corinth was a significant event that exacerbated tensions between Athens and Corinth, contributing to the widening divide between Athens and Sparta and their respective allies. This conflict showcased the complex dynamics and shifting alliances within the Greek world leading up to the Peloponnesian War.

Corcyra, an island city-state located in the Ionian Sea, had a long-standing rivalry with Corinth, its neighbor and a powerful member of the Peloponnesian League. Corinth sought to assert its influence over Corcyra and gain control of its strategic location and naval resources. However, Corcyra resisted Corinthian domination and sought support from Athens.

In 433 BC, the conflict between Corcyra and Corinth escalated, and Corcyra appealed to Athens for assistance. Athens, viewing Corinth's growing power as a threat, saw an opportunity to weaken its rival and extend its influence. Athens decided to intervene on the side of Corcyra, providing military aid and naval support.

Athens' intervention in the Corcyraean conflict marked a significant escalation of tensions between Athens and Corinth. By aligning with Corcyra, Athens openly challenged Corinth's influence and demonstrated its willingness to support its allies against Peloponnesian League members. This move further strained the relationship between Athens and Corinth, deepening the divide between the two city-states and their respective allies.

The Corcyraean conflict also highlighted the intricate web of alliances and shifting allegiances within the Greek world. Corinth, feeling threatened by Athens' support for Corcyra, sought to rally other members of the Peloponnesian League to its cause. This further polarized the Greek city-states and set the stage for a broader conflict between Athens and Sparta, drawing in their respective allies.

The involvement of Athens in the Corcyraean conflict signaled the deepening divide between Athens and Sparta and their allies. It showcased the expanding sphere of influence of both powers and their willingness to support and protect their allies against rival city-states. The conflict served as a precursor to the larger-scale conflict of the Peloponnesian War, emphasizing the growing animosity and competition between Athens and Corinth and setting the stage for the subsequent military confrontations that would follow.

3.5 Athens' Imperial Overreach:

Athens' expansionist policies and the transformation of the Delian League into an Athenian empire played a crucial role in shaping the dynamics of the Peloponnesian War. As Athens gained power and influence, it faced increasing resistance and resentment from other Greek city-states. The perception of Athens as an overreaching imperial power contributed to the growing anti-Athenian sentiment and the alignment of various city-states with Sparta.

The Delian League, initially established as a defensive alliance against the Persian threat, gradually evolved into an Athenian-dominated confederation. Athens, under the leadership of statesmen like Pericles, utilized the resources and naval capabilities of the league to strengthen its own position and extend its influence over the member states. The league's treasury was moved to Athens, and Athens assumed a more assertive role in decision-making and policy enforcement.

As Athens' power grew, so did concerns among other city-states about the erosion of their autonomy and independence. Athens' imperial ambitions and the perceived domineering behavior of its leaders created an atmosphere of mistrust and resentment. The imposition of tribute and the enforcement of Athenian control over league members further fueled these sentiments.

Many city-states saw Athens' actions as a threat to the delicate balance of power in Greece. They feared that Athens would continue to expand its influence, erode their own autonomy, and establish a hegemonic rule over the region. This perception pushed several city-states towards alignment with Sparta, viewing it as a counterbalance to Athenian power.

The growing anti-Athenian sentiment and the alignment with Sparta were crucial factors in shaping the dynamics of the Peloponnesian War. City-states such as Corinth, Megara, and Thebes, among others, actively sought to challenge Athens' dominance and saw Sparta as their natural ally in this endeavor. They believed that Sparta's military strength and its commitment to preserving the autonomy of Greek city-states would provide a counterweight to Athens' imperial ambitions.

Athens' imperial overreach, coupled with the fears of other city-states regarding the erosion of their independence, contributed to the deepening divisions and animosity between Athens and its adversaries. This perception of Athens as an imperial power seeking to dominate Greece was a significant catalyst for the outbreak of the Peloponnesian War, as it fueled the desire among several city-states to challenge and resist Athenian hegemony.

3.6 Spartan Fear of Athens:

Sparta, known for its conservative society and emphasis on military prowess, held deep apprehensions about the growing power and influence of Athens. These fears were rooted in Spartan aversion to radical change and the perceived threat Athens posed to the established order of the Greek world. The combination of Athens' expanding empire and its democratic ideals heightened Spartan hostility towards its rival.

Sparta valued stability, tradition, and the preservation of existing social and political structures. The conservative nature of Spartan society dictated that any disruption to the established order was seen as a potential threat. Athens, with its ambitious expansionist policies and the transformation of the Delian League into an Athenian empire, represented a departure from the status quo that Sparta sought to uphold.

The Spartan elite, known as the Spartiates, regarded Athens' imperialistic tendencies with suspicion. They saw Athens as a power-hungry city-state that sought to dominate and control the Greek world. Athens' growing influence over the Delian League, coupled with its assertive behavior towards other city-states, only reinforced Spartan concerns about Athenian hegemony.

Furthermore, the democratic ideals and institutions of Athens were fundamentally different from the Spartan system of government, which was based on a dual kingship and an oligarchic council. The radical democratic system in Athens, with its emphasis on citizen participation and decision-making, was seen as a potential threat to the traditional Spartan way of life. Sparta feared that Athenian democracy could inspire discontent and social unrest within its own society.

The fear of Athens' imperialism and democratic ideals served as a driving force behind Spartan hostility towards Athens. The Spartans believed that the expansionist policies and democratic ideology of Athens posed a direct challenge to their own values and way of life. The Spartan leadership sought to preserve their own power and influence while countering the perceived threat from Athens.

This fear of Athens, combined with the desire to protect the established order of the Greek world, played a significant role in shaping Spartan policy and the decision to confront Athens in the Peloponnesian War. It fueled the determination of

Sparta and its allies to challenge Athenian hegemony and safeguard their own interests and traditions.

3.7 Diplomatic Maneuverings:

In the lead-up to the Peloponnesian War, both Athens and Sparta engaged in diplomatic maneuverings to secure allies and support for their respective causes. Understanding the importance of alliances and external backing, both city-states employed different strategies to strengthen their positions and gather anti-opponent forces.

Athens, as the dominant naval power and the head of the Delian League, had a significant advantage in terms of diplomatic leverage. It used its naval superiority, economic resources, and cultural appeal to forge alliances and maintain its dominance over other city-states. Athens employed a persuasive diplomacy approach, emphasizing the benefits of alignment with the Athenian Empire. The Athenians offered protection, trade opportunities, and participation in the democratic decision-making process as incentives for other city-states to join their cause.

Athens, under the leadership of influential statesmen like Pericles, recognized the importance of soft power and the ability to sway public opinion in its favor. They promoted Athens' cultural and intellectual achievements, projecting the city-state as a beacon of civilization and progress. This cultural diplomacy aimed to win over potential allies who sought to align themselves with Athens' prestige and intellectual prowess.

On the other hand, Sparta relied on its reputation as a military powerhouse and its network of alliances within the Peloponnesian League. Sparta's military strength and reputation as the defender of Greek traditions and values provided a strong foundation for its diplomatic efforts. Spartan diplomats sought to gather anti-Athenian forces under their banner, presenting themselves as the protectors of Greek autonomy and the antidote to Athenian imperialism.

Sparta leveraged its influence over the Peloponnesian League, a coalition of city-states in the Peloponnese region, to rally support against Athens. It appealed to the fear and resentment that many city-states harbored towards Athenian dominance and used this sentiment to build alliances.

3.8 The Debate over Intervention:

The escalating tensions between Athens and Sparta prompted internal debates and divisions within the city-states themselves regarding intervention in conflicts and alliances with either power. These debates reflected the diverse political interests and factions present within each city-state, further complicating the already intricate situation.

In Athens, as a democratic city-state, the decision-making process involved discussions and debates among its citizens. The Athenian assembly, consisting of eligible male citizens, played a central role in shaping foreign policy. Within this assembly, different factions emerged, each advocating for a particular approach towards the brewing conflict. Some Athenians believed in maintaining a cautious stance and avoiding direct confrontation with Sparta, advocating for peaceful resolutions and diplomatic negotiations. Others, led by influential figures such as Pericles, championed a more assertive approach, emphasizing Athens' naval strength and the need to protect its interests and allies.

The debate over intervention in conflicts and alliances was not limited to Athens alone. In other Greek city-states, similar internal divisions emerged. Each city-state had its own political interests, aspirations, and concerns, which influenced their decisions regarding intervention. Some city-states feared the dominance of either Athens or Sparta and sought to maintain a delicate balance of power by avoiding direct involvement. Others were swayed by persuasive diplomacy or existing alliances and aligned themselves with one of the two powers.

These internal debates and divisions further heightened the complexities of the situation. The diverse political interests and factions within each city-state contributed to the fragmentation of Greece, with different city-states taking varying positions on intervention and alliances. The result was a fractured Greek world, with shifting loyalties and conflicting interests, which exacerbated the tensions between Athens and Sparta.

The internal debates and divisions over intervention underscored the challenges faced by Greek city-states in navigating the complex web of alliances and conflicts. The decisions made by each city-state had a significant impact on the course of events, shaping the alliances formed and ultimately contributing to the outbreak of the Peloponnesian War.

Conclusion: Tensions between Athens and Sparta prior to the Peloponnesian War were driven by territorial disputes, economic conflicts, ideological differences, and the fear of one another's growing power. The Megarian Decree, the Corcyraean conflict, and the imperial ambitions of Athens all contributed to the fraying relationship between the two city-states. These underlying causes set the stage for the escalation of hostilities and the eventual outbreak of the Peloponnesian War, which we will explore further in subsequent chapters.

Chapter 4: The Corinthian War: The Events Leading up to the Outbreak of Hostilities

Introduction: The Corinthian War serves as a critical precursor to the Peloponnesian War, escalating tensions between Athens and Sparta and their respective allies. This chapter explores the series of events that unfolded, leading to the outbreak of hostilities and setting the stage for the larger conflict.

4.1 The Thirty Years' Peace:

Following the First Peloponnesian War (460-445 BC), Athens and Sparta recognized the need for a period of stability and negotiated a peace treaty known as the Thirty Years' Peace in 446 BC. This treaty aimed to establish guidelines for resolving conflicts and maintain a delicate balance of power between the two major Greek city-states.

The Thirty Years' Peace was negotiated with the assistance of Pericles, an influential statesman and general from Athens, and King Pleistoanax of Sparta. The treaty set out several provisions to prevent further escalation of hostilities and promote peaceful coexistence. Key elements of the treaty included the return of conquered territories and the restoration of the status quo ante bellum, effectively rolling back territorial gains made by both Athens and Sparta during the First Peloponnesian War.

The treaty also outlined a dispute resolution mechanism, whereby conflicts arising between Athens and Sparta or their respective allies would be resolved through arbitration. This mechanism aimed to prevent the immediate resort to military action and provide a means for peaceful negotiation and settlement.

Furthermore, the Thirty Years' Peace established a non-interference clause, prohibiting Athens and Sparta from interfering in each other's allies and spheres of influence. This provision sought to limit the expansionist ambitions of both city-states and mitigate the potential for further conflicts.

The peace treaty was initially seen as a significant achievement, providing a respite from the hostilities and setting a framework for resolving disputes. However, despite its intentions, the Thirty Years' Peace proved to be fragile and ultimately failed to prevent the outbreak of the Peloponnesian War.

Over the course of the thirty-year period, tensions between Athens and Sparta persisted. Both city-states continued to pursue their own interests and engage in actions that violated the spirit of the peace treaty. Athens' growing dominance and imperialistic policies, as well as Sparta's concerns over Athenian power, gradually eroded the fragile peace. Disputes, conflicts, and the changing dynamics of power eventually led to the breakdown of the Thirty Years' Peace and the resumption of open hostilities between Athens and Sparta in 431 BC, marking the beginning of the Peloponnesian War.

The Thirty Years' Peace serves as a reminder of the challenges of maintaining long-term peace and stability in a region characterized by intense rivalries and conflicting interests. Despite its initial hopes, the treaty was unable to prevent the deeper underlying tensions between Athens and Sparta from resurfacing, ultimately leading to one of the most significant conflicts in ancient Greek history.

4.2 The Megarian Dispute:

The Corinthian War, a conflict that took place from 395 to 387 BC, was sparked by a series of disputes and tensions between Athens and Corinth. One significant trigger of the war was a dispute over the city of Megara, which became a point of contention between the two major Greek powers.

Megara, situated strategically between Athens and the Peloponnese, had long-standing trade ties with Corinth, its neighboring city-state. However, as the power dynamics in Greece shifted, Megara found itself increasingly vulnerable to Corinthian aggression. Seeking protection, Megara turned to Athens, which seized the opportunity to extend its influence and counter Corinth's dominance.

Athens, recognizing the strategic importance of Megara, formed an alliance with the city-state, offering military and political support. This alliance between Athens and Megara infuriated Corinth and deepened the existing animosity between Athens and Corinth.

The Athenian alliance with Megara further strained relations between the two major powers due to the underlying tensions and competition for influence in the region. Corinth, a prominent member of the Peloponnesian League, resented Athens' growing power and saw the Athenian-Megarian alliance as a direct challenge to its interests.

The dispute over Megara became a flashpoint, escalating the already simmering tensions between Athens and Corinth. It served as a catalyst for the Corinthian War, as both Athens and Corinth mobilized their forces and sought alliances with other Greek city-states to support their respective positions.

The Megarian dispute highlighted the intricate web of alliances, territorial disputes, and power struggles that characterized the Greek world at the time. It demonstrated how a seemingly local conflict could rapidly escalate into a larger-scale war, drawing in other city-states and sparking wider hostilities.

The Corinthian War, which ensued from the Megarian dispute, had far-reaching consequences for Greece. It not only involved Athens and Corinth but also drew in various other city-states, leading to a complex and protracted conflict. The war altered the balance of power in Greece and marked a significant turning point in the history of the region.

The Megarian dispute serves as an example of how territorial conflicts and strategic alliances could have far-reaching implications, shaping the course of events and ultimately leading to larger-scale conflicts in ancient Greece.

4.3 The Battle of Tanagra:

The Battle of Tanagra, which took place in 457 BC, was a significant military engagement between Athens and its allies against Corinth and its allies during the early stages of the First Peloponnesian War (460-445 BC). The battle resulted in a victory for Corinth and its allies, altering the dynamics of power and prompting Athens to reassess its strategy in the region.

At the time, Athens, under the leadership of Pericles, was expanding its influence and actively engaging in conflicts and alliances with various city-states. Seeking to counter Corinth's growing power, Athens formed alliances with Megara, Boeotia, and Phocis, among others, to challenge Corinthian dominance in the region.

The Battle of Tanagra was fought between the Athenian-led Delian League and the forces of Corinth and its allies. The exact details of the battle are not extensively documented, but it is believed to have taken place near the city of Tanagra in Boeotia.

Despite Athens' formidable naval strength, the battle proved to be a setback for the Athenians. Corinth and its allies emerged victorious, inflicting significant losses on the Athenian forces. The defeat at Tanagra was a blow to Athens' ambitions and highlighted the military prowess of Corinth and its allies.

The Battle of Tanagra had important implications for the strategic balance in Greece. It demonstrated that Athens, despite its naval dominance, was not invincible on land. The defeat forced Athens to reassess its approach and tactics in the ongoing conflict with the Peloponnesian League.

Following the battle, Athens shifted its focus from direct military confrontation to consolidating its power through diplomatic and economic means. The Athenians recognized that their strength lay in their naval capabilities and sought to leverage their dominance at sea to secure alliances and exert influence over other city-states.

The Battle of Tanagra marked a significant turning point in the First Peloponnesian War. It highlighted the military capabilities of Corinth and its allies and prompted Athens to adopt a more cautious and strategic approach in its pursuit of power and dominance in Greece.

The battle serves as a reminder of the complex and ever-changing dynamics of ancient Greek warfare. It demonstrates that victories and defeats on the battlefield had a profound impact on the course of the Peloponnesian War, shaping alliances, strategies, and the ultimate outcome of the conflict.

4.4 The Formation of the Delian League:

Amidst the growing threat from Corinth and other Peloponnesian allies, Athens took steps to consolidate its power and secure its dominance by transforming the Delian League into an Athenian empire. This significant development had far-reaching consequences for the political landscape of ancient Greece.

The Delian League, initially formed in 478 BC as a defensive alliance against the Persian Empire, comprised various city-states in the Aegean region. The League's headquarters were located on the island of Delos, and member states contributed ships or financial resources to the common cause.

Over time, Athens gradually assumed a leadership role within the Delian League due to its naval prowess and growing influence. As the League's power and resources increased, Athens began to assert greater control and influence over member states, effectively transforming the alliance into an Athenian empire.

One key aspect of this transformation was the relocation of the League's treasury from Delos to Athens. By centralizing the funds in Athens, the city-state gained direct control over the financial resources of the League. This move allowed Athens to finance its own military endeavors, strengthen its navy, and assert its authority over member states.

With the treasury under its control, Athens also started demanding tribute payments from member states. These tributes, intended initially for the defense against the Persians, gradually became a means for Athens to fund its ambitious building projects, such as the construction of the Parthenon and other grand structures that adorned the city.

The transformation of the Delian League into an Athenian empire had profound implications for the balance of power in Greece. As Athens gained more control over the member states, its dominance and influence extended beyond military matters to political and economic spheres.

This expansion of Athenian power and the centralization of resources and authority within Athens created tensions and resentment among member states that perceived Athens' actions as overreach and a threat to their autonomy. Some city-states resented the tribute payments and perceived Athens' actions as a form of exploitation.

The transformation of the Delian League into an Athenian empire marked a significant shift in the power dynamics of ancient Greece. Athens, through its naval strength and political maneuvering, had established itself as the dominant force in the region, exerting control over the Aegean and beyond.

The formation of the Athenian empire set the stage for the subsequent conflicts and rivalries that would culminate in the Peloponnesian War. The increasing power and influence of Athens, coupled with the growing resentment from other city-states, laid the foundation for the tensions that would eventually erupt into open hostilities.

The transformation of the Delian League into an Athenian empire demonstrates the complexities of power, ambition, and the pursuit of dominance in the ancient world. It serves as a crucial precursor to the Peloponnesian War, highlighting the underlying causes and motivations that would shape the course of the conflict.

4.5 The Megarian Decree and Sparta's Response:

In 432 BC, Athens took a significant step that further heightened tensions between the city-state and its rivals by enacting the Megarian Decree. This decree imposed economic sanctions on Megara, a key ally of Corinth and a member of the Peloponnesian League. The Megarian Decree had far-reaching implications and played a crucial role in the lead-up to the outbreak of the Peloponnesian War.

The Megarian Decree was a punitive measure by Athens aimed at weakening Megara and undermining Corinth's influence in the region. Megara, located strategically between Athens and the Peloponnese, held close ties with Corinth, making it an important ally for the city-state. By imposing economic sanctions on Megara, Athens sought to weaken Corinth's position and disrupt its alliances.

The exact reasons behind Athens' decision to enact the Megarian Decree are a subject of debate among historians. Some suggest that it was driven by economic motivations, as Athens aimed to control trade routes and undermine Corinthian economic interests. Others argue that it was a political move to assert dominance and provoke Corinth into a confrontation.

Regardless of the precise motivations, the Megarian Decree had severe consequences. The economic sanctions placed significant strain on Megara, impacting its trade and economy. Corinth, feeling threatened by Athens' actions, saw an opportunity to rally support from other Peloponnesian states, particularly Sparta, by accusing Athens of violating the terms of the Thirty Years' Peace.

Corinth's appeal to Sparta was based on the claim that the Megarian Decree violated the provisions of the peace treaty. According to Corinth, Athens' actions constituted an act of aggression and a breach of the agreed-upon terms of peaceful coexistence. Corinth sought Sparta's intervention and support in confronting Athens and defending its interests.

Sparta, as the leader of the Peloponnesian League and a traditional rival of Athens, was inclined to listen to Corinth's grievances. The Spartans, who valued stability and the preservation of the existing order, viewed Athens' growing power and influence with suspicion. They saw the Megarian Decree as evidence of Athens' expansionist ambitions and a threat to the delicate balance of power.

Sparta's response to the Megarian Decree marked a significant escalation in the tensions between Athens and Sparta. It set in motion a series of diplomatic exchanges, ultimatums, and countermeasures that ultimately led to the outbreak of the Peloponnesian War. The confrontation between Athens and Sparta, with Corinth and its allies in tow, became inevitable as both sides entrenched themselves in their respective positions.

The Megarian Decree and Sparta's response demonstrate the fragile nature of interstate relations in ancient Greece. Small disputes and acts of aggression could quickly escalate into full-scale conflicts, as each city-state sought to defend its interests and maintain its standing in the Greek world.

The Megarian Decree and the subsequent response from Sparta marked a crucial turning point in the lead-up to the

Peloponnesian War. It highlighted the deep-rooted mistrust and rivalry between Athens and Sparta and their respective allies. The economic sanctions imposed by Athens and the accusation of treaty violation by Corinth laid the groundwork for the larger conflict that would consume the Greek world for the next several decades.

4.6 The Epidamnian Affair:

The Corinthian War, which ultimately led to the Peloponnesian War, was not solely driven by tensions between Athens and Sparta. It was also influenced by conflicts in other regions that exacerbated the rivalry between the two major powers. One such conflict was the Epidamnian Affair, which played a role in escalating hostilities between Athens and Corinth.

Epidamnus, a city located in Illyria (modern-day Durres in Albania), found itself embroiled in a power struggle between different factions. One faction, supported by Corinth, sought to gain control of the city. In response, the opposing faction reached out to Athens for assistance. This presented a dilemma for Athens, as it had to consider its obligations under the existing peace treaty with Sparta, known as the Thirty Years' Peace.

The Athenians deliberated on whether to intervene in the Epidamnian conflict. On one hand, they had concerns about violating the terms of the peace treaty and provoking Corinth, a major power and a key ally of Sparta. On the other hand, they faced pressure to support the faction in Epidamnus that sought their aid.

Despite the potential risks, Athens ultimately made the decision to intervene in the Epidamnian Affair. This move can be attributed to several factors. First, Athens saw an opportunity to expand its influence in the region and counter Corinthian power. By assisting the faction opposing Corinth, Athens could establish a foothold in Illyria and gain a strategic advantage.

Second, there were internal political considerations within Athens. The influential statesman Pericles, who advocated for Athenian expansion and imperialism, supported intervention in Epidamnus. His influence and persuasive rhetoric played a significant role in swaying public opinion and convincing the Athenians to take action.

Athens' decision to intervene in Epidamnus further fueled Corinthian resentment and solidified the growing rift between the two city-states. Corinth saw Athens' actions as a direct challenge to its authority and influence in the region. This, combined with other grievances and disputes, pushed Corinth to seek support from its allies, including Sparta.

The Epidamnian Affair highlighted the complexities of interstate relations in ancient Greece. It demonstrated how conflicts in peripheral regions could be used as a pretext for larger confrontations between major powers. The involvement of Athens in Epidamnus strained its relationship with Corinth, paving the way for the Corinthian War.

The intervention in Epidamnus, despite its relatively small scale, had significant implications for the course of the Corinthian War. It further deepened the animosity between Athens and Corinth, solidifying their positions as opposing forces in the wider conflict. The Epidamnian Affair contributed to the deteriorating diplomatic landscape in ancient Greece and set the stage for the larger confrontations to come.

In conclusion, the Epidamnian Affair was a contributing factor to the Corinthian War. Athens' decision to intervene in the conflict, despite concerns about violating the peace treaty, heightened tensions with Corinth and paved the way for larger confrontations between the two city-states. The affair exemplifies how regional conflicts could become catalysts for wider conflicts in the intricate web of alliances and rivalries in ancient Greece.

4.7 The Battle of Sybota:

The Battle of Sybota, which took place in 433 BC, was a significant engagement that escalated tensions between Athens and Sparta and marked a turning point in the balance of power in ancient Greece. While officially a conflict between Corinth and Corcyra, it quickly transformed into a proxy war between Athens and Sparta due to their respective alliances.

Corcyra, a powerful naval city-state and ally of Athens, was involved in a territorial dispute with Corinth, a member of the Peloponnesian League led by Sparta. Seeking to gain an advantage, Corcyra sought the support of Athens, while

Corinth turned to Sparta for assistance. As a result, what began as a local conflict soon drew in the major Greek alliances, pitting Athens against Sparta in a proxy battle.

The battle itself took place near the small island of Sybota off the coast of Corcyra. The Athenian fleet, led by Phormio, engaged the Corinthian fleet commanded by the Corinthian admiral Aristeus. Despite being outnumbered, Phormio skillfully maneuvered his ships and won a decisive victory, sinking several Corinthian vessels and capturing others. The defeat of Corinth's navy at Sybota was a significant blow to Corinth and its Peloponnesian allies, and it marked a shift in the balance of power in favor of Athens.

The outcome of the battle had far-reaching consequences. It demonstrated Athens' naval superiority and bolstered its confidence in challenging the Spartan-led Peloponnesian League. The victory also further strained the already tense relations between Athens and Sparta, as Sparta perceived Athens' support for Corcyra as an aggressive move that threatened its own influence in the region.

The Battle of Sybota heightened the overall hostility and suspicion between Athens and Sparta, laying the groundwork for the larger conflict that would later erupt into the Peloponnesian War. It underscored the proxy nature of the conflict, where smaller city-states aligned with Athens or Sparta often found themselves embroiled in larger battles driven by the ambitions and rivalries of the two major powers.

In conclusion, the Battle of Sybota served as a catalyst for the escalation of tensions between Athens and Sparta, as it transformed a local dispute into a proxy conflict between the two major Greek alliances. The Athenian victory demonstrated their naval prowess and shifted the balance of power in the region. This pivotal event heightened suspicions and set the stage for the larger-scale conflict that would unfold in the Peloponnesian War.

4.8 The Corinthian Congress and the Outbreak of War:

In the year 432 BC, Corinth, driven by its deepening resentment towards Athens, hosted a congress of its allies. The purpose of this gathering was to rally support and build a coalition of city-states to confront Athens and challenge its growing power. Known as the Corinthian Congress, this assembly became a crucial event leading to the outbreak of the Corinthian War.

Representatives from various Peloponnesian states, including Corinth, Megara, and other anti-Athenian factions, convened in Corinth to discuss their grievances against Athens and strategize their response. The grievances ranged from Athens' imperialistic policies, perceived violations of the Thirty Years' Peace, and Athens' support for Corcyra in the Battle of Sybota. The congress provided an opportunity for Corinth to present its case against Athens and garner support for military action.

During the congress, Corinth skillfully appealed to the fears and concerns of its allies, emphasizing the need to curb Athens' expansionism and protect the autonomy of the Greek city-states. The delegates deliberated on various measures to counter Athens' dominance, including economic sanctions, naval cooperation, and the formation of a united front against the Athenian Empire.

The congress concluded with a formal declaration of war against Athens, effectively marking the outbreak of the Corinthian War. This declaration signaled a significant escalation in hostilities between the two major Greek powers and their respective alliances. The Corinthian War would come to involve a wide range of city-states, drawing them into the conflict and reshaping the political landscape of ancient Greece.

The outbreak of the war was met with mixed reactions among the Greek city-states. Some states, particularly those with long-standing grievances against Athens, eagerly joined the Corinthian-led coalition. Others, however, were more hesitant, recognizing the potential risks and consequences of engaging in a protracted conflict against the powerful Athenian Empire. The Corinthian Congress and the subsequent declaration of war set in motion a series of events that would define the course of the Peloponnesian War.

In conclusion, the Corinthian Congress held in 432 BC served as a critical turning point in the lead-up to the Corinthian War. It provided a platform for Corinth to rally its allies, present its grievances against Athens, and ultimately declare war. The congress formalized the hostility between the two major Greek powers, Athens and Corinth, and their respective alliances, setting the stage for a prolonged and destructive conflict that would shape the history of ancient Greece.

Conclusion: The Corinthian War emerged from a combination of territorial disputes, the Megarian Decree, conflicts in Epidamnus and Corcyra, and the growing animosity between Athens and Corinth. The battle of Sybota and the Corinthian Congress further solidified the confrontation, leading to the declaration of war. These events set the stage for the larger Peloponnesian War that would soon follow, plunging Greece into a protracted and devastating conflict, as we will explore in subsequent chapters.

Chapter 5: The Archidamian War Begins: Spartan Invasion of Attica and Athenian Defensive Strategy

Introduction: With the outbreak of the Peloponnesian War, the conflict quickly escalated into the Archidamian War, named after King Archidamus II of Sparta. This chapter focuses on the initial phase of the war, examining the Spartan invasion of Attica and the Athenian defensive strategy in response.

5.1 Spartan Invasion of Attica:

In 431 BC, tensions between Athens and Sparta reached a boiling point, leading to the outbreak of the Peloponnesian War. As part of their military strategy, Sparta, under the command of King Archidamus II, launched a significant invasion into Attica, the territory surrounding Athens. The invasion had several objectives, primarily aimed at weakening Athens economically, disrupting its agricultural production, and provoking a direct confrontation.

The Spartan invasion of Attica was a land-based campaign that sought to exploit Athens' vulnerability and deal a blow to its resources and morale. King Archidamus II, recognizing the importance of Attica as the heartland of Athens, planned to target its agricultural areas, which supplied the city-state with food and resources. By ravaging the countryside, burning crops, and plundering resources, the Spartans aimed to deprive Athens of its vital sustenance and disrupt its economy.

The invasion had a twofold purpose. Firstly, it aimed to weaken Athens' economic capabilities, as the city-state heavily relied on the agricultural productivity of Attica. The destruction of crops and the disruption of trade routes would put a strain on Athens' food supply and weaken its ability to sustain its population and military.

Secondly, the Spartan invasion of Attica was intended to provoke Athens into a direct confrontation. By openly attacking the Athenian territory, Sparta aimed to lure Athens' military forces out of their defensive position and engage them in battle. The Spartans hoped that a decisive victory on land would not only weaken Athens' military strength but also bolster their own reputation and undermine Athenian morale.

The invasion of Attica had a profound impact on the Athenian population. Thousands of Athenians, including women, children, and the elderly, sought refuge within the city walls of Athens, which were heavily fortified. The dense population within the city created challenging living conditions, leading to the spread of diseases such as the infamous Plague of Athens.

However, despite the devastation caused by the Spartan invasion, Athens did not engage in a direct land battle with the Spartans. Instead, the Athenians adopted a defensive strategy, relying on their powerful navy to maintain control of the sea and harass Spartan supply lines. This strategy, devised by Pericles, aimed to exhaust the Spartans and avoid a costly engagement on land, where Sparta held the advantage.

The Spartan invasion of Attica was a significant event in the early stages of the Peloponnesian War. It set the tone for the conflict, illustrating the brutal realities of warfare and the devastating impact it had on the civilian population. The invasion highlighted the contrasting strengths and weaknesses of the two city-states, with Sparta relying on its land-based military might and Athens utilizing its naval superiority and defensive strategy.

In conclusion, the Spartan invasion of Attica in 431 BC was a crucial development in the Peloponnesian War. It aimed to weaken Athens economically, disrupt its agricultural production, and provoke a direct confrontation. The invasion had a profound impact on the Athenian population, forcing them to seek refuge within the city walls. The Athenians, under the leadership of Pericles, adopted a defensive strategy, relying on their navy to counter the Spartan invasion. The invasion set the stage for the protracted conflict between Athens and Sparta and shaped the subsequent course of the war.

5.2 Athenian Defensive Strategy:

In response to the Spartan invasion of Attica in 431 BC, Athens implemented a defensive strategy under the leadership of Pericles, the prominent Athenian statesman. This strategy involved the construction and utilization of the "Long Walls" and a concentration of the population within the fortified city of Athens.

Pericles recognized the limitations of Athens' land-based military capabilities compared to Sparta's formidable hoplite infantry. To mitigate the risk of direct confrontation on land, Pericles proposed the abandonment of the rural areas of Attica, including farmland and smaller settlements, and the consolidation of the Athenian population within the fortified city walls.

The centerpiece of this defensive strategy was the construction of two parallel walls, known as the "Long Walls," which connected Athens to its port city of Piraeus and the harbor of Phaleron. These walls stretched approximately 6.4 kilometers (4 miles) and provided a protected corridor for the movement of people, supplies, and communication between Athens and its major harbors.

By concentrating the population within the fortified city, Athens aimed to protect its citizens from the devastating effects of the Spartan invasion. The fortified walls provided a strong defense against land-based attacks, while the proximity to the sea ensured access to supplies and reinforcements through the Athenian navy.

The Athenian defensive strategy relied heavily on the power and mobility of their navy. Athens possessed a dominant naval force, which was considered one of its greatest strengths. The navy safeguarded the supply lines connecting Athens to its vital grain routes from the Black Sea region, ensuring the city's food security and sustaining its empire.

Through their naval superiority, the Athenians aimed to maintain control of the sea, harass Spartan supply lines, and engage in naval battles to weaken Spartan forces. The Athenian navy was instrumental in protecting the movement of goods and maintaining communication with the empire's subject states, which provided vital resources and tribute.

The concentration of the population within the city walls, combined with the reliance on the navy for supply lines, defined Athens' defensive strategy during the early stages of the Peloponnesian War. The strategy aimed to exhaust the Spartan forces by avoiding a decisive land battle, protecting the Athenian population, and leveraging Athens' naval supremacy.

While the defensive strategy allowed Athens to safeguard its population and maintain control over its empire, it also posed challenges. The dense population within the city walls resulted in overcrowding, leading to unsanitary conditions and the outbreak of diseases such as the Plague of Athens, which further weakened the Athenian population and military.

Additionally, the defensive strategy meant that Athens had to rely heavily on its navy and maintain a robust network of alliances to sustain its empire. Any disruption in naval control or the loss of key allies could severely impact Athens' supply lines and overall strategic position.

In conclusion, the Athenian defensive strategy during the Peloponnesian War centered around the construction of the "Long Walls" and the concentration of the population within the fortified city of Athens. This strategy aimed to protect the Athenian population from the Spartan invasion and relied on the power and mobility of the Athenian navy to maintain supply lines and sustain the empire. The defensive approach allowed Athens to withstand the initial onslaught but also presented challenges such as overcrowding and reliance on naval dominance.

5.3 Pericles' Strategy of Attrition:

Pericles, the influential Athenian statesman, devised a strategy of attrition during the early stages of the Peloponnesian War. Recognizing the military superiority of Sparta's hoplite forces on land, Pericles advocated for a cautious approach that focused on avoiding direct confrontations and instead relied on Athens' naval dominance to undermine Sparta's strength.

Pericles understood that engaging in open field battles against the highly disciplined and formidable Spartan hoplites would likely result in heavy losses for Athens. Instead, he sought to exhaust the Spartans through a war of attrition, leveraging Athens' naval supremacy and conducting raids on the Peloponnesian coast.

Athens possessed a powerful navy, which was one of its greatest assets. Pericles recognized that by using the navy to disrupt Spartan supply lines and undermine their economy, Athens could gradually weaken the Spartan war effort and force them to expend resources in defense of their territories.

Under Pericles' strategy, Athenian naval forces would conduct regular raids along the Peloponnesian coast, targeting key coastal cities and Spartan-controlled regions. These raids aimed to disrupt trade, hinder agricultural production, and inflict economic damage on the Spartan allies.

By focusing on naval raids, Athens aimed to create a sense of insecurity and economic instability among the Spartans and their allies. The disruption of supply lines and the loss of valuable resources would gradually erode the Spartan war effort, weakening their resolve and diminishing their military capabilities.

Pericles' strategy of attrition was not without risks and challenges. The reliance on naval raids meant that Athens needed to maintain a strong and well-equipped navy capable of sustained operations. It required an effective command structure, skilled naval commanders, and a network of allies to support these endeavors.

Furthermore, the strategy of attrition required patience and endurance from the Athenian population. Pericles emphasized the importance of maintaining unity and resilience in the face of prolonged conflict, urging the citizens to endure the hardships of war while relying on the city's defensive walls and its maritime strength.

Pericles' strategy of attrition aimed to wear down the Spartans through a combination of economic disruption, psychological pressure, and the preservation of Athens' military resources. The objective was to avoid unnecessary risks in direct land battles while gradually undermining the Spartan war effort.

While Pericles' strategy achieved some success in the early years of the war, it also faced challenges and limitations. The outbreak of the Plague of Athens in 430 BC severely weakened Athens, including the loss of Pericles himself. The strategy of attrition alone could not prevent the eventual decline of Athens' fortunes and the ultimate defeat in the Peloponnesian War.

During the early years of the Peloponnesian War, Athens was struck by a devastating plague in 430 BC. The exact nature of the disease is uncertain, but it is believed to have been typhoid fever or a similar infectious illness. The plague had a profound impact on Athens, causing widespread suffering, death, and social upheaval.

The outbreak of the plague in Athens had severe consequences for the city and its population. The crowded and unsanitary conditions within the city walls provided an ideal environment for the rapid spread of the disease. The Athenians, who had taken refuge behind their defensive Long Walls, found themselves vulnerable to the epidemic.

The plague had a significant impact on the morale and psychological well-being of the Athenian population. The sudden and indiscriminate nature of the disease created fear and despair among the citizens. The Athenians, who had previously believed in the invincibility of their city and its empire, were now confronted with their own mortality and the fragility of their society.

The epidemic also took a toll on Athens' military strength. The loss of manpower due to illness weakened the Athenian forces, making it more challenging to sustain their naval raids and defend their territories. The absence of capable leaders, including the death of Pericles himself, further exacerbated the situation.

The plague's impact on Athens went beyond the immediate physical and military consequences. It also had political repercussions. The social fabric of the city was disrupted as people grappled with the loss of loved ones and the breakdown of societal norms. The crisis created a climate of uncertainty and led to a shift in leadership and strategy.

With the loss of Pericles, a new generation of leaders emerged, each with their own perspectives and priorities. These leaders, including Cleon and Nicias, adopted different approaches to the war and sought to navigate the challenges posed by the plague and the ongoing conflict with Sparta.

Despite the hardships caused by the plague, Athens did not succumb immediately. The city managed to survive and even launched successful military campaigns in subsequent years. However, the plague had a lasting impact on Athens' ability to sustain its war effort and maintain its dominance. It weakened the city's military capabilities, strained its resources, and undermined the confidence and unity of its citizens.

The plague of Athens stands as a somber reminder of the devastating impact of disease on a society at war. It serves as a turning point in the course of the Peloponnesian War, marking a shift in the balance of power and the fortunes of Athens. The city would continue to face significant challenges in the years to come, ultimately leading to its eventual defeat at the hands of Sparta.

5.5 Cleon and the Change in Athenian Strategy: After Pericles' death, the influential statesman Cleon emerged as a prominent figure in Athenian politics. Cleon advocated for a more aggressive approach, pushing for offensive operations against Sparta and its allies. This shift marked a departure from Pericles' strategy of attrition. After the death of Pericles, the influential Athenian statesman Cleon rose to prominence in Athenian politics. Cleon's emergence marked a shift in Athenian strategy, moving away from Pericles' strategy of attrition and adopting a more aggressive approach towards Sparta and its allies.

Cleon was known for his strong and assertive personality, as well as his persuasive oratory skills. He believed that Athens should take advantage of its naval superiority and launch offensive operations against Sparta and its allies. Cleon argued that a more proactive approach would not only weaken Sparta but also enhance Athens' standing and potentially bring about a swift victory.

Under Cleon's influence, Athens pursued a more aggressive military strategy. The Athenians engaged in expeditions and campaigns aimed at exerting control over Spartan allies, capturing important territories, and undermining Spartan influence. Cleon believed that by taking the fight to Sparta and its allies, Athens could secure a decisive advantage and force a favorable resolution to the war.

One notable example of Cleon's assertive strategy was the successful Athenian expedition to the island of Sphacteria in 425 BC. Led by Cleon himself, the Athenians managed to capture a significant number of Spartan soldiers, which was a major blow to Sparta's military reputation.

Cleon's approach, however, was not without controversy. His aggressive tactics and uncompromising stance often drew criticism from more cautious and moderate voices within Athens. Critics accused Cleon of recklessness and endangering Athenian lives for personal gain. Nevertheless, Cleon remained a powerful force in Athenian politics and continued to shape the city's military strategy during the war.

Cleon's tenure as a leading figure in Athenian politics was cut short by his death in 422 BC during the Battle of Amphipolis. His demise marked the end of an era characterized by his confrontational style and assertive strategy. Subsequent Athenian leaders, such as Nicias, would adopt different approaches and seek diplomatic solutions to the ongoing conflict.

The shift in Athenian strategy under Cleon reflected a departure from Pericles' more cautious and defensive approach. Cleon's aggressive stance aimed to exploit Athens' naval power and achieve a decisive victory over Sparta. While his tactics were not always universally popular, Cleon's influence left a lasting impact on Athenian military strategy during the later stages of the Peloponnesian War.

5.6 Spartan Siege of Plataea: In 429 BC, the Spartans laid siege to the city of Plataea, an ally of Athens. Plataea held out against the Spartan forces for several years, becoming a symbol of resistance and a drain on Spartan resources. In 429 BC, the Spartans initiated a siege on the city of Plataea, which had remained a staunch ally of Athens. The siege of Plataea became a protracted and significant event in the Peloponnesian War, lasting for several years and resulting in a prolonged struggle between the Spartan forces and the defenders of the city.

Plataea, strategically located in Boeotia, posed a threat to Spartan interests in the region. Its allegiance to Athens and its resistance to Spartan dominance made it a target for the Spartan forces, who sought to quell any opposition and secure their control over Boeotia.

The Spartans, known for their formidable land-based military, surrounded Plataea and initiated a siege. The objective was to cut off the city from external support, starve its population, and ultimately force their surrender. The Spartans deployed various tactics, including blockades, attacks on supply lines, and continuous assaults on the city's defenses.

However, the Plataeans displayed remarkable resilience and determination in the face of the Spartan siege. They managed to hold out against the superior Spartan forces for an extended period, much longer than anticipated. The defenders of Plataea, driven by a strong sense of loyalty to Athens and a desire for freedom, fiercely resisted the Spartan assaults and endured the hardships of the siege.

The siege of Plataea not only showcased the resolve and determination of the city's defenders but also became a symbol of resistance against Spartan hegemony. The prolonged resistance of Plataea became a drain on Spartan resources and military manpower, diverting their attention and efforts from other fronts.

The siege continued for several years until 427 BC when the Spartans finally managed to breach the city's defenses and capture Plataea. The surviving defenders were either killed or taken captive, and the city was demolished, erasing it from the map. The fall of Plataea marked a significant victory for Sparta and a blow to Athens and its allies.

Despite its ultimate defeat, the siege of Plataea left a lasting legacy in the annals of the Peloponnesian War. The courage and tenacity displayed by the Plataean defenders resonated throughout Greece and inspired other city-states in their resistance against Spartan dominance. The siege also highlighted the high costs and challenges of sieges in ancient warfare, as the Spartans struggled to overcome the determined resistance of the Plataeans.

5.7 Continuing Spartan Invasions and Athenian Responses: Throughout the early years of the war, the Spartans periodically invaded Attica, causing damage and displacing the rural population. Athens continued to rely on its defensive strategy, reinforcing its Long Walls and relying on naval power to sustain its empire. Throughout the early years of the Peloponnesian War, the Spartans launched periodic invasions into Attica, the territory surrounding Athens. These invasions aimed to weaken Athens economically, disrupt its agricultural production, and force a direct confrontation. The Spartan hoplites devastated the countryside, burning crops, and plundering resources.

In response to these Spartan invasions, Athens adhered to its defensive strategy. The Athenians concentrated their population within the fortified city of Athens, relying on the protection of their Long Walls, which connected Athens to its port at Piraeus. By abandoning the rural areas of Attica, Athens sought to minimize the damage caused by Spartan incursions and preserve its military strength.

The Long Walls served as a vital lifeline for Athens, enabling the city to maintain contact with its port and sustain its empire through maritime trade. Athens heavily relied on its powerful navy, which was the backbone of its military might and played a crucial role in safeguarding supply lines and protecting its interests across the Aegean Sea.

By reinforcing the Long Walls and fortifying the city of Athens, the Athenians aimed to deter direct land battles with the superior Spartan hoplites. They recognized that engaging in open field battles against the Spartans would likely result in significant losses. Instead, Athens chose to focus on its naval superiority and embarked on offensive operations against Spartan territories and allies, conducting raids along the Peloponnesian coast to disrupt Spartan supply lines and undermine their economy.

The Athenian strategy of relying on their naval power and conducting raids rather than engaging in direct land battles was influenced by the ideas of Pericles and his successors, who believed in the importance of avoiding costly conflicts on Spartan terms. This defensive strategy, coupled with offensive naval operations, aimed to wear down the Spartans and their allies through attrition, limiting their ability to launch decisive attacks on Athens itself.

While the Athenians' defensive approach provided some security and preserved their empire, it also came with challenges. The concentration of the population within the city walls made Athens susceptible to overcrowding and the outbreak of diseases, such as the devastating plague that struck in 430 BC. Additionally, relying on maritime trade made Athens vulnerable to blockades and naval losses, as any significant disruption to their navy could have severe consequences for their supply lines and overall war effort.

Nonetheless, Athens maintained its defensive strategy and naval dominance for a significant portion of the war, leveraging its strengths and mitigating the impact of Spartan invasions. However, as the war progressed and new leaders emerged, including Cleon, the Athenians would adopt more aggressive and risky strategies, leading to significant shifts in the course of the conflict.

5.8 The Peace of Nicias: In 421 BC, a temporary peace known as the Peace of Nicias was negotiated between Athens and Sparta. This brought a temporary halt to hostilities, providing a respite from the ravages of war. However, the peace was short-lived, as tensions soon resurfaced. In 421 BC, a temporary peace agreement known as the Peace of Nicias was negotiated between Athens and Sparta. The peace was named after the Athenian general Nicias, who played a significant role in the negotiations. The Peace of Nicias aimed to bring a temporary halt to hostilities and restore a sense of stability to the Greek world.

Under the terms of the peace agreement, both Athens and Sparta agreed to return any captured territories and prisoners of war. The city-states also pledged to uphold a truce for a duration of fifty years. The peace agreement was seen as an opportunity to ease the suffering and devastation caused by the long years of war and provide an opportunity for reconstruction and recovery.

However, the Peace of Nicias proved to be short-lived. The underlying tensions and rivalries between Athens and Sparta, as well as their respective allies, were not fully resolved. The peace agreement did not address the fundamental issues that had led to the conflict in the first place, such as territorial disputes, power struggles, and ideological differences. As a result, it was only a matter of time before tensions resurfaced and the war reignited.

Moreover, the peace was marked by various violations and incidents that eroded trust between the two sides. Both Athens and Sparta accused each other of violating the terms of the peace, leading to escalating tensions and renewed hostilities. The Peace of Nicias ultimately failed to provide a lasting solution to the deep-rooted conflicts between the two major powers of ancient Greece.

The breakdown of the Peace of Nicias would lead to a new phase of the Peloponnesian War, marked by renewed hostilities and shifting alliances. The war would continue for several more years, with both Athens and Sparta striving for dominance and seeking to assert their respective interests in the Greek world.

Conclusion: The Archidamian War began with the Spartan invasion of Attica and Athens' adoption of a defensive strategy. Pericles' strategy of attrition and the reliance on the navy to sustain the empire marked the early stages of the conflict. The devastating plague and the subsequent shift in leadership under Cleon added further complexity to Athenian decision-making. Despite Spartan invasions and ongoing challenges, Athens managed to hold its ground through defensive measures and naval operations. The Peace of Nicias brought a temporary pause in the conflict, but the war would resume with renewed intensity. The subsequent chapters will delve into the evolving dynamics of the war and its lasting impact on ancient Greece.

Chapter 6: Pericles and the Athenian Empire: The Influence of Athens over Its Allies

Introduction: During the Peloponnesian War, Athens emerged as a dominant power, establishing and maintaining control over its empire. This chapter focuses on the leadership of Pericles and the extent of Athenian influence over its allies within the Delian League.

6.1 Pericles: The Athenian Statesman: Pericles, an influential statesman and general, played a pivotal role in shaping Athens' policies and strategies during the war. Known for his oratory skills and political acumen, Pericles was a champion of Athenian democracy and imperial ambitions. Pericles was indeed a central figure in Athenian politics and military affairs during the Peloponnesian War. He belonged to the aristocratic Alcmaeonid family and emerged as one of the most prominent statesmen of his time. Pericles held various important positions in Athens, including serving as a general and leading figure in the city's democratic government.

Pericles is best known for his influential speeches and his role in shaping Athenian policies. He emphasized the importance of democracy and believed in the power of the people to govern themselves. Pericles championed the idea of Athens as a cultural and intellectual center, promoting the arts, philosophy, and literature. Under his leadership, Athens experienced a golden age of prosperity and cultural achievements.

During the war, Pericles advocated for a defensive strategy and the concentration of the population within the safety of Athens' city walls. This strategy, known as the "Long Walls," aimed to protect the citizens of Athens from Spartan invasions and relied on Athens' naval supremacy for sustenance and trade. Pericles recognized the limitations of the Athenian army against the superior Spartan hoplites and sought to avoid direct confrontations on land.

However, Pericles' strategy faced challenges, particularly when the devastating plague struck Athens in 430 BC. The plague, which claimed the lives of many Athenians, including Pericles himself, weakened the city both militarily and psychologically. With Pericles' death, the Athenian leadership underwent changes, and a more aggressive approach, led by figures like Cleon, began to emerge.

Despite his passing, Pericles' influence continued to shape Athens and its conduct during the war. His emphasis on democracy, cultural achievements, and the defense of Athens' empire left a lasting legacy. Pericles' speeches and ideas were recorded by Thucydides, providing valuable insights into his vision and the political climate of the time.

Overall, Pericles' leadership and political acumen played a significant role in shaping Athens' policies and strategies during the Peloponnesian War, leaving an indelible mark on the city's history and the course of the conflict.

6.2 The Delian League: The Delian League, initially formed as a defensive alliance against the Persian Empire, became an instrument of Athenian hegemony. Athens transformed the league into an empire under its control, asserting dominance over member states and using their resources to strengthen its own position. The Delian League underwent a transformation from a defensive alliance to an Athenian empire during the Peloponnesian War. Originally established in 478 BC as a coalition of Greek city-states to counter the Persian threat, the Delian League was led by Athens, which emerged as the dominant power within the alliance.

Under Athenian leadership, the Delian League achieved several military victories against the Persians and successfully expelled them from the Aegean region. However, Athens gradually exerted more control over the league and its resources, eventually transforming it into an empire.

Athens relocated the treasury of the Delian League from the island of Delos to Athens, consolidating financial control. The league's member states, originally contributing ships or monetary contributions for the common defense, gradually became subjects of Athenian domination. Athens used the league's resources, including its fleet, to enforce its own interests and assert its hegemony over the Aegean region.

Athens imposed tributes and taxes on the league's members, using the funds to finance its ambitious building projects, such as the construction of the Parthenon and the strengthening of its navy. The Athenian empire expanded its influence and established administrative control over numerous city-states in the region.

However, this transformation of the Delian League into an Athenian empire was not universally accepted or welcomed. Some member states resented Athens' dominance and the imposition of tribute payments. These grievances, along with Athens' aggressive actions and growing imperial ambitions, contributed to the resentment and eventual rebellion of some of the league's members, further fueling the flames of the Peloponnesian War.

The transformation of the Delian League into an Athenian empire represents a significant development in the context of the Peloponnesian War. Athens' pursuit of its own interests and the use of the league's resources for its own benefit deepened the divide between Athens and its allies, fostering tensions and contributing to the conflict's escalation.

It's worth noting that the shift from a defensive alliance against Persia to an Athenian empire had profound consequences not only for the Peloponnesian War but also for the power dynamics and balance of power in ancient Greece as a whole. The rise of the Athenian empire and the assertion of Athenian hegemony set the stage for the conflicts and rivalries that ultimately led to the outbreak of the Peloponnesian War.

6.3 Athenian Control and Tribute: Athens exercised direct control over the Delian League's treasury, which was relocated from Delos to Athens. Member states were required to pay tribute to Athens, both in the form of monetary contributions and military service. This tribute solidified Athenian economic and military power. Athens, as the leader of the Delian League, exerted significant control over the league's treasury and imposed tribute requirements on its member states. The relocation of the treasury from Delos to Athens symbolized the growing dominance of Athens in the league's affairs.

Member states of the Delian League were obligated to make regular tribute payments to Athens. These tribute payments took the form of monetary contributions or goods, which Athens used to finance its own activities and projects. The exact amount of tribute varied depending on the size and resources of each member state.

The tribute system served multiple purposes for Athens. First, it provided a steady source of revenue that allowed Athens to fund its ambitious building projects, maintain a powerful navy, and strengthen its military capabilities. Second, the tribute system solidified Athens' economic power and influence over the league's member states, as they became financially dependent on Athens.

Additionally, the tribute system served as a means for Athens to exercise control and enforce its dominance within the league. Failure to pay tribute or resistance to Athenian authority could result in punitive measures, such as military intervention or the imposition of harsher tribute requirements.

By controlling the league's treasury and imposing tribute obligations, Athens consolidated its economic and military power, further strengthening its position as the leading city-state in the Delian League. However, this dominance and imposition of tribute payments also fueled resentment among some member states, contributing to the eventual conflicts and rebellions that erupted during the Peloponnesian War.

6.4 Oligarchic Governments and Athenian Interference: In many member states of the Delian League, Athens intervened in their internal affairs, often dismantling oligarchic governments and replacing them with democratic regimes that were more amenable to Athenian influence. This interference sparked resentment and resistance from some allies. Athens did intervene in the internal affairs of certain member states of the Delian League, particularly those that exhibited oligarchic or pro-Spartan tendencies. Athens sought to establish democratic regimes in these states, which were more aligned with Athenian interests and more likely to support Athenian policies.

This interference in the internal governance of member states was driven by a combination of strategic and ideological motivations. Strategically, Athens aimed to ensure that its allies were loyal and supportive, as well as prevent potential uprisings or alliances with Sparta. By promoting democratic governments, Athens believed it could maintain control and prevent the rise of oligarchic factions that might challenge its authority or align with its enemies.

Ideologically, Athens viewed democracy as the superior form of government and saw it as their mission to spread democratic ideals throughout Greece. They believed that democratic governments would be more receptive to Athens' leadership and policies, as they shared similar values and principles.

However, this interference often sparked resentment and resistance among the affected states. The imposition of democratic governments by Athens was seen by some as an infringement on their autonomy and as an unwanted intrusion into their internal affairs. In many cases, Athens faced opposition and even rebellions from these states, as they sought to regain their independence and shake off Athenian control.

The interference in the internal affairs of member states, along with the imposition of democratic governments, contributed to the growing discontent and dissatisfaction with Athenian dominance within the Delian League. This, in turn, fueled the anti-Athenian sentiment that eventually led to rebellions and conflicts within the league during the Peloponnesian War.

6.5 Athenian Colonization and Settlements: As part of its imperial policy, Athens established colonies and settlements in strategically important regions. These new settlements served as a means of expanding Athenian control and projecting its influence further into the Aegean. As part of its imperial policy, Athens engaged in a program of colonization and establishment of settlements in various regions. These new colonies and settlements served several purposes for Athens.

Firstly, they provided strategic outposts that extended Athenian control and influence over key areas. These strategic locations often included islands, coastal regions, and important trade routes. By establishing colonies in these areas, Athens could exert its power and secure its interests more effectively, both economically and militarily. These settlements acted as bases for naval operations, facilitating control over trade routes and projecting Athenian power throughout the Aegean Sea.

Secondly, these colonies served as a means of relieving population pressure within Athens itself. The establishment of new settlements offered Athenian citizens opportunities for land ownership, trade, and a fresh start in areas with potential for growth and prosperity. This allowed for the expansion of Athenian influence while also addressing domestic concerns such as unemployment and overcrowding.

Thirdly, the establishment of colonies and settlements allowed Athens to exploit the resources of these regions. These resources could include fertile land for agriculture, mines for valuable minerals, or access to lucrative trade routes. By controlling these resources, Athens could enhance its economic strength and sustain its imperial ambitions.

Overall, Athenian colonization and the establishment of settlements played a significant role in expanding Athenian control, securing strategic positions, alleviating domestic pressures, and exploiting economic opportunities. These actions were instrumental in solidifying Athens' imperial power and dominance over the Aegean region, ultimately contributing to the tensions and conflicts that arose during the Peloponnesian War.

6.6 Cultural and Intellectual Dominance: Athens, renowned for its cultural and intellectual achievements, exerted significant soft power over its allies. The city-state's intellectual and artistic dominance attracted scholars, philosophers, and artists from across the Greek world, solidifying Athens' cultural influence. Athens was renowned for its cultural and intellectual achievements, which played a significant role in solidifying its influence and soft power over its allies in the Delian League. Athens was a center of intellectual and artistic excellence, attracting scholars, philosophers, and artists from various parts of the Greek world.

Athens boasted a vibrant intellectual and cultural scene, with prominent thinkers such as Socrates, Plato, and Aristotle contributing to the development of philosophy and intellectual discourse. The city-state was also home to famous playwrights like Aeschylus, Sophocles, and Euripides, who produced timeless works of drama. The artistic accomplishments of Athenian sculptors, architects, and painters were renowned, exemplified by magnificent structures like the Parthenon on the Acropolis.

The intellectual and artistic achievements of Athens created a magnetic effect, drawing scholars and artists from other Greek city-states to the city. This influx of talent and ideas contributed to the cultural vibrancy and intellectual atmosphere of Athens. The presence of renowned philosophers, playwrights, and artists helped establish Athens as a hub of knowledge, creativity, and innovation, reinforcing its cultural dominance.

Moreover, Athens used its cultural and intellectual achievements as a means of promoting its own political and ideological agenda. The city-state's democratic ideals and values were intertwined with its cultural identity. Athens presented itself as the epitome of democratic governance and intellectual enlightenment, projecting these values to its allies in the Delian League.

The cultural and intellectual dominance of Athens not only enhanced its prestige but also served as a tool for influencing and shaping the attitudes and beliefs of its allies. The allure of Athens' cultural and intellectual scene, combined with its political and military power, created a compelling image of Athens as a leading force in the Greek world. This cultural influence and soft power played a crucial role in maintaining the loyalty and support of its allies, even in the face of increasing tensions and conflicts during the Peloponnesian War.

6.7 Democratic Ideals and Imperialism: Athens promoted democratic ideals within its empire, encouraging its allies to adopt democratic forms of government. While this may have been presented as a noble aspiration, it also served to consolidate Athenian control and ensure loyalty from its allies. Athens promoted democratic ideals within its empire as part of its imperial strategy. While the Athenians presented their push for democratic governance as a noble aspiration, it also served to consolidate their control over the Delian League and ensure loyalty from their allies.

Athens, as a proud democracy, believed in the superiority of its political system and saw it as a model for other city-states to follow. They saw spreading democracy as a means to foster stability, unity, and fairness within their empire. By encouraging their allies to adopt democratic forms of government, Athens aimed to create a network of like-minded states that would align with its interests and support its imperial ambitions.

However, it is important to note that Athens' promotion of democracy was not purely altruistic. The Athenians recognized that democratic governments were more likely to be sympathetic to their rule and less inclined to challenge Athenian authority. Democratic governments, based on the participation of the citizenry, were perceived to be more manageable and easier to control compared to oligarchic or tyrannical regimes. By encouraging democratic governance, Athens sought to shape the political landscape of its empire in a way that was conducive to its own interests.

Additionally, promoting democracy allowed Athens to portray itself as a champion of freedom and equality, serving as a justification for its imperial actions. By associating its empire with democratic values, Athens sought to legitimize its dominance and garner support from its allies. It presented its imperial project as a mission to spread democracy and protect the interests of the Greek world against external threats.

While Athens did encourage democratic reforms in some allied states, it is important to recognize that its promotion of democracy was selective and driven by self-interest. Athens did not hesitate to intervene in the internal affairs of its allies, dismantling oligarchic governments and installing democratic regimes that were more favorable to Athenian control. This interference in the political systems of its allies, under the guise of promoting democracy, allowed Athens to further consolidate its power and maintain a firm grip on its empire.

In essence, Athens' promotion of democratic ideals within its empire was a strategic move to consolidate its control, ensure loyalty, and project a favorable image. While there were undoubtedly genuine proponents of democracy within Athens, the imperial context in which these ideals were promoted cannot be ignored.

6.8 Opposition and Revolts: Despite Athens' efforts to maintain control, there were instances of opposition and revolts from some member states. The most notable example is the revolt of Samos in 440 BC, which challenged Athenian authority and required military intervention to suppress. Despite Athens' attempts to maintain control over its empire, there were instances of opposition and revolts from some member states. The revolt of Samos in 440 BC is a notable example of such resistance against Athenian authority.

Samos, an island located in the eastern Aegean Sea, was a member of the Delian League and subject to Athenian control. However, Samos had a strong navy and a degree of autonomy within the league. The Samians resented Athenian interference and sought greater independence.

In 440 BC, the Samians rebelled against Athens and sought to break free from its control. They refused to pay tribute and challenged Athenian authority. The Samian revolt posed a significant threat to Athenian hegemony, as it had the potential to inspire other member states to follow suit.

In response, Athens launched a military intervention to suppress the revolt. The Athenians deployed their navy and besieged the island of Samos, seeking to regain control by force. The siege lasted for several years, with Athens ultimately emerging victorious.

The Samian revolt and its subsequent suppression by Athens demonstrated the limits of Athenian control and the potential for resistance within its empire. It revealed the underlying tensions and grievances that existed among some member states, even those that had been part of the Delian League for a significant period.

The revolt of Samos serves as a reminder that not all member states of the Athenian empire were content with Athenian dominance. It highlights the inherent challenges of maintaining control over a diverse and geographically scattered empire. While Athens was able to suppress the revolt, such uprisings showcased the ongoing struggle between imperial control and the desire for autonomy among the member states of the Delian League.

Conclusion: Under the leadership of Pericles, Athens established a powerful empire and exercised significant influence over its allies within the Delian League. The control of tribute, interference in internal affairs, establishment of colonies, and cultural dominance all contributed to Athenian hegemony. While Athens promoted democratic ideals, the imperialistic nature of its rule and the resistance from some member states exposed the complexities and challenges of maintaining control over a vast empire. The evolving dynamics between Athens and its allies would continue to shape the course of the Peloponnesian War and its aftermath.

Chapter 7: The Plague of Athens: The Devastating Impact of Disease on Athenian Society

Introduction: One of the most significant events during the Peloponnesian War was the outbreak of a devastating plague that struck Athens. This chapter delves into the nature of the plague, its impact on Athenian society, and the ensuing consequences.

7.1 The Arrival of the Plague: In 430 BC, the plague, believed to be typhoid fever or a similar infectious disease, reached Athens through its bustling port, Piraeus. It spread rapidly, taking hold within the crowded city and affecting people from all walks of life. In 430 BC, a devastating plague struck Athens, causing widespread suffering and loss of life. The exact nature of the disease is still debated among historians, but it is often believed to have been typhoid fever or a similar infectious disease.

The plague is thought to have originated from outside Athens, likely brought in by ships arriving at the city's bustling port of Piraeus. The close quarters and dense population within Athens provided the ideal conditions for the rapid spread of the disease.

The plague took a heavy toll on the Athenian population, affecting people from all social classes and backgrounds. It caused widespread illness and death, leading to a significant decline in the city's population and a loss of manpower. The impact of the plague was particularly severe because Athens had already concentrated its population within the city walls as part of its defensive strategy.

One of the notable victims of the plague was the Athenian statesman Pericles, who succumbed to the disease in 429 BC. His death was a significant blow to Athens, as he had been a key figure in leading the city-state and shaping its policies.

The arrival of the plague had a profound psychological and social impact on Athens. The high mortality rate and the suffering experienced by the population led to a sense of despair and disillusionment. People turned to religious and superstitious practices in search of answers and remedies. The breakdown of social order and the loss of faith in traditional institutions further exacerbated the challenges faced by Athens during the war.

The plague not only weakened Athens militarily but also had long-lasting effects on its society and morale. It played a significant role in shifting the course of the war and contributed to Athens' eventual defeat at the hands of Sparta.

7.2 Symptoms and Mortality: The plague brought with it a range of severe symptoms, including high fever, debilitating weakness, respiratory problems, and gastrointestinal issues. People suffered from intense pain and experienced rapid deterioration of their health. The mortality rate was alarmingly high, with a significant number of Athenians succumbing to the disease. The plague that struck Athens in 430 BC was characterized by a variety of severe symptoms, causing immense suffering among the population. The symptoms included:

High Fever: Affected individuals experienced a persistent and high-grade fever, which often persisted for days or even weeks.

Debilitating Weakness: The disease caused extreme weakness and fatigue, leaving individuals bedridden and unable to carry out their daily activities.

Respiratory Problems: Many people suffered from respiratory issues, including coughing, shortness of breath, and chest pain. Some accounts describe individuals coughing up blood or experiencing severe chest congestion.

Gastrointestinal Disturbances: The plague also brought about gastrointestinal symptoms such as nausea, vomiting, diarrhea, and abdominal pain.

Skin Lesions: Some reports mention the appearance of skin lesions or rashes, which were often a manifestation of secondary infections or complications.

Rapid Deterioration: The disease progressed rapidly in many cases, with individuals experiencing a swift decline in their health and well-being. The severity of the symptoms often led to a quick deterioration in overall physical condition.

The mortality rate of the plague was alarmingly high, with a significant number of Athenians succumbing to the disease. The exact percentage of the population affected is difficult to ascertain, as historical records vary in their estimates. However, it is widely accepted that the plague had a devastating impact on Athens, causing a significant loss of life and further exacerbating the city's already dire situation during the Peloponnesian War.

The combination of the severe symptoms, the rapid spread of the disease, and the high mortality rate contributed to the overall despair and demoralization experienced by the Athenian population during this time. It is estimated that the plague resulted in a substantial decline in Athens' population, further weakening the city-state's ability to sustain its war effort and defend itself against its enemies.

7.3 Impact on Athenian Society: The plague had a profound impact on various aspects of Athenian society. The loss of life led to a demographic crisis, with a significant decline in the population. This, in turn, affected labor, agriculture, and overall productivity.

7.4 Political and Military Consequences: The plague severely disrupted Athenian political and military affairs. Prominent figures, including Pericles himself, succumbed to the disease, resulting in a leadership vacuum and a shift in political dynamics. The loss of capable leaders and soldiers weakened Athens' military capabilities, providing an opportunity for its enemies to exploit. The political and military consequences of the plague in Athens were significant:

Leadership Vacuum: The plague claimed the life of Pericles, one of Athens' most prominent statesmen and military strategists. His death left a leadership void in Athens, as he had been a key figure in shaping the city-state's policies and strategies. The loss of such a capable leader during a critical time of war created a challenge for Athens in finding suitable successors to navigate the ongoing conflict.

Political Instability: The death of Pericles and other influential figures during the plague created political instability in Athens. With the loss of experienced statesmen, factions and rivalries emerged as different individuals and groups vied for power and influence. This internal turmoil further weakened Athens' ability to effectively manage the war and respond to its enemies.

Weakening of Military Capabilities: The plague also took a toll on Athens' military strength. The loss of soldiers and experienced military leaders had a detrimental effect on the city-state's ability to maintain its forces and conduct military operations. The decrease in manpower weakened Athens' army, making it more vulnerable to attacks and less capable of mounting effective offensives against its enemies.

Opportunistic Actions by Enemies: The weakened state of Athens due to the plague provided an opportunity for its enemies, particularly Sparta and its allies, to exploit the situation. Recognizing Athens' vulnerabilities, they seized the chance to launch attacks and capitalize on the city-state's weakened military and political position. This further added to Athens' challenges and contributed to its declining fortunes in the war.

In summary, the plague had significant political and military consequences for Athens. The loss of capable leaders, political instability, and a weakened military allowed Athens' enemies to take advantage of the situation. These factors contributed to the difficulties faced by Athens in effectively responding to the ongoing conflict and maintaining its power and influence in the face of adversity.

7.5 Social Disruption and Psychological Impact: The plague created immense social disruption, as families and communities were torn apart by illness and death. Traditional mourning and burial rituals were compromised due to the overwhelming number of deaths. The psychological toll on the survivors was immense, leading to fear, despair, and a sense of hopelessness. The plague had profound social disruption and a significant psychological impact on the people of Athens:

Social Disruption: The rapid spread of the plague in Athens led to widespread social disruption. Families were torn apart as loved ones fell ill and died, leaving behind grieving relatives. The sheer number of deaths overwhelmed the city's resources, making it difficult to handle proper burials and rituals. The usual customs and practices surrounding death and mourning were disrupted, adding to the sense of chaos and despair.

Breakdown of Social Structures: The plague challenged the social fabric of Athenian society. The disease's indiscriminate nature affected people from all walks of life, regardless of social status or wealth. This resulted in a breakdown of social structures and hierarchies as the disease affected both the wealthy and the poor. The loss of family members and friends disrupted social networks, leading to a sense of isolation and vulnerability.

Psychological Impact: The psychological impact of the plague was immense. The fear of contracting the disease and witnessing its devastating effects created a pervasive sense of anxiety and despair among the population. The overwhelming number of deaths and the constant exposure to suffering and loss took a toll on the mental well-being of the survivors. The psychological trauma caused by the plague left a lasting impact on the collective memory of the Athenians and influenced their attitudes and behavior during and after the war.

Erosion of Trust: The plague's impact on Athenian society also eroded trust and cooperation among the population. The fear and suspicion generated by the disease led to a breakdown in social bonds, as people became wary of close contact with others for fear of contagion. This erosion of trust further contributed to the sense of isolation and psychological distress experienced by the Athenians.

In summary, the social disruption and psychological impact of the plague in Athens were significant. The breakdown of social structures, the disruption of mourning rituals, and the psychological trauma experienced by the survivors all contributed to a sense of despair and hopelessness. These factors further complicated the challenges faced by Athens during the war and added to the overall toll of the devastating epidemic.

7.6 Medical Response and Athenian Resilience: Athens, with limited medical knowledge and resources, struggled to combat the disease. Despite their best efforts, medical practitioners were unable to effectively treat or prevent the spread of the plague. However, the Athenians displayed remarkable resilience and solidarity, with individuals and communities coming together to support and care for the afflicted. Athens faced significant challenges in responding to the plague due to limited medical knowledge and resources. The Athenians, like many ancient societies, did not have a comprehensive understanding of infectious diseases or access to effective treatments. As a result, their efforts to combat the plague were largely futile.

However, despite these limitations, the Athenians demonstrated remarkable resilience and solidarity in the face of the epidemic. The devastating impact of the plague prompted acts of compassion and selflessness within the community. Individuals and communities came together to provide care and support for the afflicted, often at great personal risk.

Some Athenians, particularly those who had previously survived the disease and developed immunity, volunteered to care for the sick. They showed great courage in tending to the needs of the infected, providing comfort, and easing suffering to the best of their abilities. These acts of compassion and bravery during a time of crisis exemplified the Athenian spirit and their commitment to communal well-being.

Furthermore, the plague also brought forth a sense of solidarity among the Athenians. The shared experience of suffering and loss fostered a collective resilience and a sense of unity. This solidarity helped the Athenians endure the hardships caused by the plague and the ongoing war.

While Athens struggled to combat the disease medically, the resilience and support displayed by its citizens were a testament to their strength and determination. The Athenians' ability to come together and care for one another in the face of such adversity is a testament to the human spirit and their commitment to their community.

7.7 Influence on the Course of the War: The plague had a significant impact on the trajectory of the Peloponnesian War. The weakened state of Athens provided an opportunity for its enemies, particularly Sparta, to launch further attacks and gain the upper hand. Additionally, the plague disrupted supply lines and affected the Athenian navy's ability to sustain its empire. The weakened state of Athens as a result of the plague provided its enemies, particularly Sparta and its allies, with an opportunity to gain the upper hand in the conflict.

The loss of capable leaders, including Pericles, and the overall decline in the Athenian population and military strength weakened Athens' position. This allowed Sparta to launch further attacks and invasions into Athenian territory, exploiting the vulnerability of the city-state. The Spartans, under the leadership of King Archidamus II, led a series of invasions into Attica, causing damage and disruption to the Athenian countryside.

Additionally, the plague disrupted the supply lines and logistical capabilities of Athens, including its naval power. The Athenian navy, which had been a crucial component of its empire and its ability to sustain its dominion over the Aegean, was hampered by the plague. The disease affected the sailors and weakened the manpower available for naval operations, further undermining Athens' ability to maintain control over its empire and defend its interests.

The combination of military setbacks, population decline, and logistical challenges imposed by the plague had a significant impact on the overall balance of power in the war. The weakened state of Athens provided an advantage to its adversaries, enabling them to exploit the situation and advance their own interests.

It is important to note, however, that the plague was not the sole determining factor in the outcome of the war. There were other complex political, military, and strategic factors at play. Nonetheless, the plague undoubtedly played a role in weakening Athens and shifting the dynamics of the conflict in favor of its enemies.

7.8 Historical Accounts and Thucydides: The historian Thucydides, who himself survived the plague, provided a detailed account of the disease's impact in his work, "History of the Peloponnesian War." His writings serve as a valuable source of information about the nature and consequences of the plague. Thucydides, an Athenian historian and general, witnessed the plague firsthand and provided a detailed account of its impact in his monumental work, "History of the Peloponnesian War." Thucydides' writings are an invaluable source of information for our understanding of the nature and consequences of the plague that struck Athens during the war.

Thucydides describes the symptoms of the disease, the rapid spread of the contagion, and the devastating effect it had on the population. His vivid descriptions capture the physical and psychological suffering endured by the Athenians. Thucydides also provides insights into the social and political consequences of the plague, highlighting its impact on leadership, social cohesion, and the overall course of the war.

Thucydides' account is highly regarded for its accuracy and meticulous attention to detail. His work stands as a seminal historical document, not only for the study of the Peloponnesian War but also for our understanding of ancient diseases and their societal impact. Thucydides' firsthand experience of the plague lends a unique perspective to his narrative and contributes to its credibility.

It is worth noting that Thucydides' work is not without limitations. As a historian, he focused primarily on the political and military aspects of the war, and his account of the plague reflects this emphasis. Nonetheless, his writings provide valuable insights into the impact of the disease on Athenian society and its significance in the context of the Peloponnesian War.

Thucydides' "History of the Peloponnesian War" remains a foundational source for scholars studying the period, and his detailed account of the plague continues to inform our understanding of the historical and social consequences of infectious diseases in ancient times.

Conclusion: The plague of Athens during the Peloponnesian War was a catastrophic event that had far-reaching consequences. It caused widespread death, disrupted social structures, weakened Athens politically and militarily, and influenced the course of the war. The resilience and solidarity displayed by the Athenians in the face of this calamity showcased the strength of their society. The plague of Athens remains a stark reminder of the devastating impact that disease can have on even the most advanced civilizations.

Chapter 8: The Mytilenean Debate: The Moral and Political Dilemmas Faced by Athens

Introduction: During the Peloponnesian War, Athens faced moral and political dilemmas that tested the principles of its democratic system. The Mytilenean Debate is a prime example of the difficult choices Athens had to make. This chapter explores the events surrounding the Mytilenean Debate and the implications for Athenian democracy.

8.1 Background: The Rebellion of Mytilene: Mytilene, a city-state on the island of Lesbos and a member of the Athenian Empire, rebelled against Athenian rule in 428 BC. This rebellion presented Athens with a critical challenge, forcing the city-state to respond and determine the fate of Mytilene. The rebellion of Mytilene was a significant event during the Peloponnesian War that took place in 428 BC. Mytilene, a city-state located on the island of Lesbos in the Aegean Sea, was a member of the Athenian Empire and subject to Athenian rule. However, growing discontent and dissatisfaction with Athenian control led to a full-scale rebellion.

The exact reasons for the rebellion are not fully clear, but it is believed that the Mytilenians were motivated by a desire for greater autonomy and resentment towards Athenian dominance. They likely saw an opportunity to break free from

Athenian control amidst the ongoing conflict with Sparta and its allies.

8.2 Athenian Response: Upon learning of the rebellion, Athens faced a crucial decision regarding how to respond to the Mytilenian revolt. Initially, there were different opinions within the Athenian assembly. Some advocated for harsh reprisals and the complete destruction of Mytilene as a deterrent to other potential uprisings. Others argued for a more moderate approach, suggesting that only the leaders of the rebellion should be punished while sparing the general population.

8.3 The Debate: The debate over the fate of Mytilene was heated and reflected the larger tension between maintaining control over the empire and ensuring its stability. Cleon, a prominent Athenian politician known for his aggressive stance, argued for the complete annihilation of Mytilene as an example to other subject cities. However, Diodotus, a more moderate voice, argued against such drastic measures, emphasizing the importance of keeping subject states within the empire.

8.4 Decision and Reversal: Initially, the Athenian assembly voted in favor of Cleon's proposition, which called for the execution of all adult males in Mytilene and the enslavement of the women and children. However, the decision caused a wave of remorse and second thoughts among the Athenians. The next day, the assembly reconvened, and Diodotus successfully argued for a reversal of the previous decision.

8.5 The Consequences: The Athenians ultimately decided to send a new ship to countermand the order for mass executions. However, they still punished the leaders of the rebellion and imposed heavy financial and political penalties on Mytilene. This event highlighted the complexities of ruling over an empire and the delicate balance Athens needed to strike between maintaining control and avoiding excessive brutality that could alienate its allies.

The rebellion of Mytilene had significant implications for Athens' relationship with its subject states and the stability of the Athenian Empire. It served as a reminder of the challenges and complexities of maintaining control over a vast empire during a time of war.

8.6 The Revocation of the Death Sentence: Despite initial support for Cleon's proposition, the assembly ultimately voted to revoke the death sentence on the Mytileneans. This decision was based on Diodotus' argument and a subsequent second vote that allowed citizens to reconsider their initial choice. After the initial decision to execute all adult males in Mytilene, the Athenian assembly reconvened and voted to revoke the death sentence. This reversal was indeed influenced by the arguments put forth by Diodotus, who appealed to the assembly to reconsider the harsh punishment and emphasized the importance of maintaining their reputation for fairness and justice.

Diodotus argued that executing the entire population of Mytilene would set a dangerous precedent and could lead other subject cities to revolt out of fear of a similar fate. He emphasized that Athens should strive for a reputation as a just and merciful ruler, as this would make it easier to retain control over its empire in the long run. Diodotus also highlighted the potential loss of valuable resources and manpower that could result from the mass execution.

The assembly allowed citizens to reconsider their initial vote, and after hearing Diodotus' arguments and reflecting on the consequences of their decision, the majority of the Athenians voted in favor of revoking the death sentence. This decision demonstrated the capacity of the Athenian democratic system to rectify hasty or unjust decisions and showed a willingness to consider alternative perspectives.

Instead of executing all Mytilenean males, Athens punished the leaders of the rebellion and imposed severe financial and political penalties on the city. This allowed Athens to assert its authority and maintain control over Mytilene while avoiding the potential backlash and negative consequences of a mass execution.

8.7 Implications and Lessons Learned: The Mytilenean Debate highlighted the moral and political dilemmas faced by Athens. It showcased the tension between the Athenian pursuit of power and the principles of justice, compassion, and democratic decision-making. The arguments put forth by Diodotus emphasized the importance of fairness, justice, and the long-term interests of the Athenian Empire. His appeals to reconsider the harsh punishment and preserve Athens' reputation for justice demonstrated the moral dilemma faced by the Athenians. The subsequent revocation of the death sentence showcased the capacity of the Athenian democratic system to rectify decisions made in haste or under the influence of strong emotions.

The Mytilenean Debate serves as a reminder of the challenges inherent in wielding power and the delicate balance between authority and morality. It highlights the complexities of governance and the need for careful consideration of the consequences of one's actions. The Athenians learned valuable lessons about the importance of maintaining a just and merciful image to retain the loyalty of their subject cities and avoid inciting further rebellions.

The Mytilenean Debate continues to resonate as a historical example of the ethical dilemmas faced by those in positions of power. It reminds us of the importance of balancing self-interest with principles of justice, compassion, and democratic decision-making, even in times of conflict and upheaval.

8.8 Impact on Athenian Democracy: The Mytilenean Debate marked a significant moment in Athenian democracy, showcasing the influence of public deliberation and the ability of citizens to reassess and correct their initial judgments. The debate also emphasized the role of influential figures like Cleon and Diodotus in shaping public opinion. The debate demonstrated the importance of public discourse and persuasion in shaping the opinions of the Athenian citizens. Influential figures like Cleon and Diodotus played pivotal roles in presenting their arguments and influencing public opinion. Cleon's initially popular proposition for the execution of all adult males in Mytilene highlighted the power of rhetoric and emotional appeals. Conversely, Diodotus' reasoned argument and call for reconsideration led to a shift in public sentiment and the ultimate revocation of the death sentence.

The Mytilenean Debate showcased the responsiveness of Athenian democracy to the changing tides of public opinion. It revealed the capacity of the citizens to reconsider their initial judgments and make decisions that aligned more closely with their democratic values. This aspect of Athenian democracy, where citizens had the ability to participate directly in decision-making and rectify hasty or ill-informed choices, distinguished it from other political systems of the time.

The debate also underscored the influence of influential individuals in shaping public opinion. Cleon and Diodotus, as prominent statesmen and orators, were able to sway the assembly with their arguments and rhetoric. Their role in the debate highlighted the power of persuasive speech and the significance of influential figures in shaping the course of Athenian democracy.

Overall, the Mytilenean Debate had a lasting impact on Athenian democracy by illustrating its capacity for open deliberation, the ability of citizens to reassess decisions, and the influence of influential figures in shaping public opinion. It served as a reminder of the complexities and nuances of democratic governance, showcasing both the strengths and vulnerabilities of the Athenian system.

8.9 Historical Reflections: Thucydides, the historian who chronicled the Peloponnesian War, provided a detailed account of the Mytilenean Debate. His writings offer insights into the political dynamics, moral considerations, and the subsequent repercussions of the decision made by the Athenian assembly. Thucydides' writings offer valuable historical reflections on the political dynamics and moral considerations surrounding the debate, as well as the repercussions of the decision made by the Athenian assembly.

Thucydides' account of the Mytilenean Debate provides us with a deeper understanding of the motivations and arguments presented by both Cleon and Diodotus. He delves into the moral and political dilemmas faced by Athens, highlighting the tension between the pursuit of power and the principles of justice and compassion.

Thucydides' narrative also sheds light on the broader implications of the Mytilenean Debate. He explores the consequences of the initial decision to execute the Mytilenean rebels and the subsequent reversal of that decision. Thucydides examines the impact of these actions on the stability of the Athenian Empire and the perceptions of Athens among its allies and enemies.

Furthermore, Thucydides' account provides insights into the complexities of political decision-making and the role of public deliberation in Athenian democracy. He portrays the influence of influential figures like Cleon and Diodotus, emphasizing their rhetorical skills and their ability to sway public opinion.

Thucydides' historical reflections on the Mytilenean Debate serve as a valuable source for understanding the political, moral, and psychological dimensions of the event. His writings provide us with a nuanced perspective on the dynamics of Athenian democracy, the challenges it faced, and the lessons that can be learned from this critical moment in history.

By studying Thucydides' account, we can gain valuable insights into the complexities of political decision-making, the impact of public deliberation, and the moral dilemmas faced by ancient societies. Thucydides' work continues to be a significant source for understanding the political, social, and moral aspects of the Mytilenean Debate and its broader implications.

Conclusion: The Mytilenean Debate exemplifies the complex moral and political dilemmas faced by Athens during the Peloponnesian War. It underscores the tension between justice and expediency, and the delicate balance between the pursuit of power and adherence to democratic principles. The decision to revoke the death sentence on the Mytileneans demonstrated the capacity of Athenian democracy to correct course and prioritize fairness. The Mytilenean Debate remains a compelling case study in moral decision-making and the challenges of governance during times of conflict.

Chapter 9: The Sicilian Expedition: Athens' Ill-Fated Campaign against Syracuse

Introduction: The Sicilian Expedition was a pivotal event in the Peloponnesian War, where Athens launched a major military campaign against Syracuse in an attempt to expand its empire. This chapter explores the motivations behind the expedition, its planning, the course of the campaign, and its disastrous outcome.

9.1 Motivations for the Sicilian Expedition: Athens sought to expand its influence and secure valuable resources by launching the Sicilian Expedition. The desire for territorial gain, access to Sicilian grain, and the weakening of Spartan allies were among the key motivations driving the Athenian decision. Athens had several motivations for launching the Sicilian Expedition. The desire for territorial gain and the acquisition of valuable resources played a significant role in Athenian decision-making. Here are some of the key motivations behind the expedition:

Territorial Expansion: Athens sought to expand its influence and control over new territories. Sicily was a rich and fertile region with numerous Greek city-states, and Athens saw an opportunity to establish dominance in the area. Conquering Sicilian cities would not only provide Athens with new territories but also weaken the influence of rival city-states, particularly Sparta.

Access to Resources: Sicily was known for its abundant agricultural resources, particularly grain. Athens, heavily reliant on grain imports to feed its population, aimed to secure a steady supply of Sicilian grain to sustain its empire and reduce its dependence on external sources.

Weakening Spartan Allies: The expedition aimed to weaken Sparta and its allies by undermining their influence in the region. By attacking Spartan allies in Sicily, Athens sought to disrupt the Spartan network and diminish their overall power in the Peloponnese.

Economic and Financial Benefits: The conquest of Sicily held the promise of significant economic and financial benefits for Athens. The wealth of Sicilian city-states, combined with potential tribute and increased trade, could bolster Athens' treasury and strengthen its position as a dominant maritime power.

Political Prestige and Nationalism: The expedition was also driven by a desire for political prestige and nationalism. Athens, as a democratic city-state, sought to showcase its military prowess and demonstrate its superiority over other Greek states. Success in Sicily would not only solidify Athens' position as a major power but also boost morale among its citizens.

It is worth noting that while the motivations for the Sicilian Expedition seemed promising on paper, the campaign ultimately proved to be a disastrous venture for Athens. The expedition ended in a military defeat, resulting in the loss of a significant portion of the Athenian fleet and a severe blow to Athenian power and morale.

9.2 Preparations and Alliances: Athens assembled a substantial force of both land and naval troops for the expedition. The city-state also formed alliances with local Sicilian cities, aiming to gain support and establish a base of operations for the campaign. The desire for territorial gain and the acquisition of valuable resources played a significant role in Athenian decision-making. Here are some of the key motivations behind the expedition:

Territorial Expansion: Athens sought to expand its influence and control over new territories. Sicily was a rich and fertile region with numerous Greek city-states, and Athens saw an opportunity to establish dominance in the area. Conquering Sicilian cities would not only provide Athens with new territories but also weaken the influence of rival city-states, particularly Sparta.

Access to Resources: Sicily was known for its abundant agricultural resources, particularly grain. Athens, heavily reliant on grain imports to feed its population, aimed to secure a steady supply of Sicilian grain to sustain its empire and reduce its dependence on external sources.

Weakening Spartan Allies: The expedition aimed to weaken Sparta and its allies by undermining their influence in the region. By attacking Spartan allies in Sicily, Athens sought to disrupt the Spartan network and diminish their overall power in the Peloponnese.

Economic and Financial Benefits: The conquest of Sicily held the promise of significant economic and financial benefits for Athens. The wealth of Sicilian city-states, combined with potential tribute and increased trade, could bolster Athens' treasury and strengthen its position as a dominant maritime power.

Political Prestige and Nationalism: The expedition was also driven by a desire for political prestige and nationalism. Athens, as a democratic city-state, sought to showcase its military prowess and demonstrate its superiority over other Greek states. Success in Sicily would not only solidify Athens' position as a major power but also boost morale among its citizens.

It is worth noting that while the motivations for the Sicilian Expedition seemed promising on paper, the campaign ultimately proved to be a disastrous venture for Athens. The expedition ended in a military defeat, resulting in the loss of a significant portion of the Athenian fleet and a severe blow to Athenian power and morale.

9.3 The Siege of Syracuse: The Athenians launched a siege of Syracuse in 415 BC. The initial stages of the campaign saw some success, as Athens secured a foothold and began laying siege to the city. However, the Syracusans, led by the brilliant general Hermocrates, proved resilient and mounted a strong defense. The Siege of Syracuse, which took place in 415-413 BC, was a critical phase of the Sicilian Expedition. Here are some key points regarding the siege:

Initial Success: The Athenians, led by generals Nicias, Demosthenes, and Alcibiades, initially achieved some success in the early stages of the siege. They secured a foothold in Sicily, established a fortified position, and began laying siege to the city of Syracuse.

Syracusan Resistance: The Syracusans, under the leadership of their general Hermocrates, proved to be formidable opponents. They mounted a strong defense, utilizing their knowledge of the local terrain to their advantage. The Syracusan navy also played a crucial role in repelling Athenian naval assaults.

Athenian Setbacks: Despite their initial gains, the Athenians encountered setbacks during the siege. Internal divisions among the Athenian leadership, particularly the recall of Alcibiades to Athens for trial, disrupted their operations and weakened their overall command.

Syracusan Counterattacks: The Syracusans, with the support of reinforcements from other Sicilian city-states and Spartan allies, launched counterattacks against the Athenians. They were successful in repelling several Athenian assaults and inflicting heavy casualties.

Failed Athenian Retreat: In 413 BC, the Athenians attempted to retreat from Syracuse by sea but were intercepted by the Syracusan navy. The Athenian fleet suffered a decisive defeat in the naval Battle of the Great Harbor, resulting in the loss of many ships and soldiers.

Athenian Defeat and Retreat: Following their defeat in the naval battle, the Athenians found themselves trapped in Syracuse. The Syracusans, with the aid of Spartan reinforcements led by General Gylippus, continued to press their advantage. The Athenians faced a desperate situation and were eventually forced to attempt a land retreat. However, they were pursued and suffered heavy losses, with the majority of their forces captured or killed.

The siege of Syracuse marked a turning point in the Sicilian Expedition and had a profound impact on Athens. The defeat dealt a severe blow to Athenian military power, depleted their resources, and diminished their confidence. It is often considered a significant factor in Athens' ultimate downfall in the Peloponnesian War.

9.4 Athenian Setbacks and Strategic Errors: Despite initial gains, the Athenians encountered setbacks and made critical strategic errors during the course of the campaign. These included the unsuccessful attempt to block the entrance to the harbor and the failure to secure crucial supplies. During the Sicilian Expedition, the Athenians indeed attempted to blockade the entrance to the harbor of Syracuse. They constructed a double wall across the mouth of the harbor as a means to cut off the city's access to supplies and reinforcements. However, the construction process faced challenges and obstacles.

The Syracusans fiercely resisted the Athenian blockade, engaging in naval skirmishes and obstructing the construction efforts. The Athenians also had to contend with adverse weather conditions, which further impeded their progress. As a result, the construction of the wall was never completed, and the harbor remained open for the Syracusan navy to receive supplies and reinforcements.

This failure to effectively blockade the harbor was a significant setback for the Athenians. It allowed the Syracusans to maintain their maritime connections, ensuring a steady flow of resources and support. The failure of the blockade undermined the Athenians' objective to isolate Syracuse and weakened their strategic position during the siege. During the siege of Syracuse, the Athenians encountered significant challenges in securing crucial supplies. The Syracusans, aided by their Spartan allies, effectively disrupted Athenian naval operations and impeded the delivery of provisions and reinforcements to the besieging forces.

The Syracusan navy engaged in regular naval skirmishes and blockades, intercepting Athenian supply ships and disrupting their supply lines. They also deployed their own fleet to control the waters around Syracuse, making it difficult for the Athenians to navigate and resupply their troops.

As a result, the Athenians faced a shortage of essential provisions, including food, water, and other necessary resources. The lack of supplies strained their ability to sustain the siege and weakened their overall position. The besieging forces were subjected to deteriorating conditions and increasing hardships, which further hindered their efforts to overcome the resilient Syracusan defenses.

The inability to secure crucial supplies was a significant strategic error on the part of the Athenians. It undermined their chances of success in the siege and contributed to their ultimate defeat in the Sicilian Expedition.

During the Sicilian Expedition, the Athenian expeditionary force faced internal divisions and conflicting strategies among its leadership. The generals in command, Nicias and Alcibiades, held differing opinions on how to proceed, leading to tensions and indecisiveness within the Athenian leadership.

Nicias, a cautious and conservative general, advocated for a more defensive approach, urging the Athenians to consolidate their position and wait for reinforcements. On the other hand, Alcibiades, a charismatic and ambitious leader, favored a more aggressive and expansionist strategy. He proposed seeking alliances with Sicilian cities and expanding Athenian influence in the region.

These differing strategies and disagreements between the two commanders created divisions within the Athenian leadership. The lack of unity and clear direction undermined the effectiveness of the campaign, as the Athenians were unable to pursue a cohesive and coordinated strategy. This internal strife and lack of consensus weakened their ability to respond effectively to the challenges posed by the Syracusan defenses.

The internal divisions and conflicting strategies among the Athenian leadership were a significant factor in the ultimate failure of the Sicilian Expedition. The inability to overcome these divisions and establish a unified command structure hindered the Athenians' ability to execute a successful campaign and contributed to their defeat.

During the siege of Syracuse, the Athenians made a critical strategic error in their attempt to capture the high ground of Epipolae. Epipolae was a key strategic position overlooking Syracuse, and its capture would have given the Athenians a significant advantage in the siege. However, the Athenian assault on Epipolae was poorly coordinated and ultimately unsuccessful.

The Athenians launched their attack on Epipolae from multiple directions but failed to synchronize their movements effectively. The lack of coordination resulted in confusion and disarray among their forces. Additionally, the difficult terrain and Syracusan resistance presented further challenges to the Athenians.

The Syracusans, led by their general Hermocrates, quickly recognized the Athenian assault and mounted a strong defense. They were able to repel the Athenian forces and inflict heavy casualties. The Athenians' failed assault on Epipolae weakened their position and allowed the Syracusans to maintain their defensive advantage.

This strategic error proved costly for the Athenians, as it hindered their ability to effectively besiege Syracuse and secure a decisive victory. It also demonstrated the importance of careful planning, coordination, and understanding of the terrain in military operations.

The arrival of Spartan reinforcements under the command of General Gylippus was a significant turning point in the Siege of Syracuse. The Spartans, renowned for their military prowess, brought fresh troops and valuable expertise to aid the Syracusans in their defense against the Athenian siege.

With the arrival of Spartan reinforcements, the Syracusans gained a considerable advantage. The Spartans brought disciplined hoplites and experienced commanders who could effectively counter the Athenian forces. Their presence bolstered the morale of the Syracusans and provided a renewed sense of determination.

The arrival of Spartan reinforcements posed a greater challenge for the Athenians. It forced them to contend with a more formidable and coordinated defense, as well as a strengthened Syracusan navy. The Spartans' military expertise and their ability to coordinate with the Syracusans disrupted Athenian plans and added complexity to the ongoing siege.

The presence of Spartan reinforcements further highlighted the significance of the conflict. It transformed the siege from a local conflict into a larger-scale confrontation between two major Greek powers, Athens and Sparta. The Athenians faced an increasingly formidable opposition, making their task of capturing Syracuse more daunting and their ultimate success less certain.

9.5 Syracuse's Counteroffensive: The Syracusans, bolstered by reinforcements from other Greek cities, launched a counteroffensive against the besieging Athenian forces. The

Syracusan navy effectively neutralized the Athenian fleet, and the Athenians found themselves trapped and facing defeat.

9.6 Athenian Retreat and Defeat: Recognizing their dire situation, the Athenians attempted a retreat. However, they faced a series of disastrous engagements and suffered heavy losses. The retreat turned into a rout, with the Syracusans pursuing and inflicting further casualties on the Athenian forces.

9.7 Consequences and Significance: The defeat of the Sicilian Expedition was a severe blow to Athens, both militarily and psychologically. The loss of a significant portion of its forces weakened Athens' naval power and depleted its resources, setting the stage for further defeats in the later years of the war.

9.8 Thucydides' Account: The historian Thucydides, an eyewitness to the events, provided a detailed account of the Sicilian Expedition in his work, "History of the Peloponnesian War." His writings offer valuable insights into the motivations, strategies, and consequences of the campaign.

9.9 Lessons Learned: The Sicilian Expedition serves as a cautionary tale about the dangers of overreaching and underestimating the capabilities of the enemy. It highlights the importance of sound military planning, effective leadership, and understanding the logistical challenges of conducting large-scale operations in unfamiliar territories.

Conclusion: The Sicilian Expedition stands as a major turning point in the Peloponnesian War and the decline of Athenian power. The Athenian desire for expansion and the ambition to secure valuable resources led to a disastrous campaign against Syracuse. The defeat dealt a severe blow to Athens, weakening its military and hastening its eventual defeat in the war. The Sicilian Expedition serves as a sobering reminder of the perils of imperial overreach and the complexities of waging war in distant lands.

Chapter 10: The Peace of Nicias: Temporary Ceasefire and Its Consequences

Introduction: Amidst the prolonged Peloponnesian War, the Peace of Nicias was a temporary ceasefire negotiated between Athens and Sparta. This chapter explores the circumstances that led to the peace agreement, its terms, the challenges in its implementation, and the subsequent consequences for both city-states.

10.1 Background: After the disastrous Sicilian Expedition, both Athens and Sparta found themselves weary and economically strained. Seeking relief from the ongoing conflict, they pursued negotiations that led to the Peace of Nicias in 421 BC.

10.2 Negotiations and Terms of the Peace: The negotiations for the peace agreement were led by the Athenian statesman Nicias and the Spartan general Pleistoanax. The terms of the peace included a mutual cessation of hostilities, the return of captured territories, and a pledge of alliance against common enemies.

10.3 Challenges in Implementing the Peace: Despite the agreement, implementing the terms of the peace proved challenging. Disagreements arose over the interpretation of certain clauses, and both sides harbored suspicions and mistrust, making it difficult to establish a lasting peace.

10.4 Internal Opposition: In both Athens and Sparta, there were factions that opposed the peace agreement. Hawks in Athens, led by Alcibiades, argued for a continuation of the war, while hardline Spartans saw the peace as a sign of weakness and pushed for a resumption of hostilities.

10.5 The Siege of Plataea: One significant event that strained the peace was the siege of Plataea. The Spartans, disregarding the peace agreement, laid siege to the city, which was an ally of Athens. The conflict further eroded trust and created tension between the two sides.

10.6 The Breakdown of Peace: The peace agreement eventually broke down due to escalating incidents and a lack of commitment from both Athens and Sparta. Violations of the peace terms, internal power struggles, and renewed ambitions for expansion led to a resumption of hostilities.

10.7 Consequences of the Peace of Nicias: The breakdown of the peace had significant consequences for Athens and Sparta. It prolonged the war and intensified the conflict, resulting in further loss of lives and resources. It also highlighted the difficulty of achieving a lasting peace in the face of deep-rooted enmity and conflicting interests.

10.8 Thucydides' Account: Thucydides, the historian of the Peloponnesian War, documented the events surrounding the Peace of Nicias. His writings provide valuable insights into the negotiations, challenges, and ultimate failure of the peace agreement.

10.9 Lessons Learned: The Peace of Nicias serves as a lesson on the complexities of achieving and maintaining peace in the midst of a protracted war. It underscores the challenges of reconciling conflicting interests, managing internal opposition, and building trust between warring factions.

Conclusion: The Peace of Nicias, though initially seen as a potential resolution to the Peloponnesian War, ultimately proved short-lived and unable to bring lasting peace between Athens and Sparta. It highlights the difficulties of negotiating and implementing peace agreements amidst deep-seated animosity and conflicting ambitions. The breakdown of the peace further prolonged the war and intensified the suffering experienced by both city-states. The Peace of Nicias serves as a cautionary tale about the fragility of peace in the midst of long-standing conflicts and the challenges of overcoming entrenched divisions.

Don't miss out!

Visit the website below and you can sign up to receive emails whenever Christoffer Smestad publishes a new book. There's no charge and no obligation.

https://books2read.com/r/B-A-DDRW-FSTJC

BOOKS 2 READ

Connecting independent readers to independent writers.

www.ingramcontent.com/pod-product-compliance
Lightning Source LLC
Chambersburg PA
CBHW051218160726
47994CB00002B/658

9 798822 360331 3